Begging for Justice

The Silent Coalition

Pamela Smith

ISBN 0-7414-5118-2

Published by:

INFINITY
PUBLISHING.COM

1094 New DeHaven Street, Suite 100
West Conshohocken, PA 19428-2713
Info@buybooksontheweb.com
www.buybooksontheweb.com
Toll-free (877) BUY BOOK
Local Phone (610) 941-9999
Fax (610) 941-9959

Printed in the United States of America

Printed on Recycled Paper

Published June 2010

Dedication

This book is dedicated to my family for the strength they have shown me during my incarceration, my rape and abuse, and all my ups and downs. They never judged me or second-guessed my quest for justice.

My husband, Eddie,
Son, Maurice,
Daughter, Lesia,
Grandson, Kyante,
Brothers, Raymond (R.L.), Leon, Jimmy and Kermit,
Three beloved sisters, Elweeder, Esther and Diana,
Beloved mother, Gladys Brannon Pinkard, my Solid Rock,
Beloved grandfather, Raymond Lee Brannon, Sr., the Pillar of the Brannon family and the first black police officer in Cushing, OK.

Thank You

I share this book with all my friends and the community that have supported me through some of the darkest times of my life. A community that came together to support me, Pamela Smith, for a Grand Jury Petition to bare my soul to the world, and to help me gather five thousand signatures to convene the Grand Jury that was a miscarriage of justice (Tulsa, OK).

Special thank you's go to former County Commissioner Mr. Wilbert Collins; Former Senator Maxine Horner; Roosevelt Milton, Local President of the NAACP-OKC; James Carpenter, Legal Regress; Esther Vaughn; Carolyn Holmes; Marion Corberetta; Camellia Clincy; Katie McClain; Dr. Steve Hoyer; Don Caldwell; Bishop Lee V. and Martha Broom; Bishop Donald O'Neal Tyler; Rev. Melvin Easiley; Pastor Greg and the late Carmetta Wilson; Irene and Larry Chance; Johnnie Johnson and a very warm and sincere thank you to Candance Rowe, victim.

Also, all the churches that supported me and allowed me to do speak-outs at their churches against prison rapes and abuse.

Pamela Smith

You may visit or contact Pamela Smith at the following:

Website: www.pamelasmith4u.com
e-mail: psrapefoundation@yahoo.com
Youtube: psrapefoundation (or enter: Rape Behind Prison Walls)

Table of Contents

CASES CITED

Constitutional and Statutory Provisions involved:
Fourteenth Amendment, Due Process
Eight Amendment, Cruel and Unusual Punishment
Sixth Amendment, Right to a Fair Trial

Federal Rules of Civil Procedures:

28 USC § 1331
28 USC § 1983
28 USC § 1367
28 USC § 1254(I)

District Court January 6-13, 2004, Tulsa, OK	No. 00-CV-035-C
Tenth Circuit Court Of Appeal Denver, CO Supplemental Brief	 No. 01-5085 No. 06-909
Grand Jury November 22, 2004 Tulsa County, Tulsa, OK	Pamela Smith and Candace Rowe
U.S. Supreme Court January 4, 2007 Washington, DC Writ Rehearing Supplemental Brief	No. 06-909

CHAPTER 1

Hi! Today I will tell you my story, my rape, my case. The Pamela Smith Story.

Growing up in Cushing, Oklahoma, I came from a family of four brothers and three sisters. I'm the seventh child of eight. My parents, Raymond and Gladys Brannon instilled all the good things they could in their children to make sure that we grew up and did everything a grownup person is supposed to do in life – make good choices, try to make good decisions. As I tell my story, you'll see that all that my parents instilled in me, my loving mother and my father, I failed by the wayside and made some bad choices. I was easily influenced by other people and pure greed. Today I will tell you my story.

I went to school at Booker T. Washington Elementary School. I later went to Cushing Junior High, then went on to Cushing Senior High. I went to school with my brother Jimmy and my sister Diana. I had a brother Leon that used to be a Dallas police officer. He passed away recently. My sister Diana, Jimmy and I were all in the same class. We were in the special education class which today they call dysfunctional children, but back then they called it special ed. There was nothing special about us other than we were special to our parents. But we got along great, my sisters and brothers and I. I finished high school in the year of 1972. I worked for Earl Gibble, an oil company in Cushing. I got married and had a son we named Maurice. I married my high school sweetheart whose name was Zelford. We lived in Cushing and stayed married close to two years. I adored my husband and my son. My son was my pride and my joy and he still is today. Maurice Smith. He belongs to God. I recall my son going through a storm of hell, I fell on my face and prayed night and day and God brought it to pass. I tell people sometimes 'You have to pray a storm away'.

My first experience in life with race was when I was growing up in Cushing. A young lady came to Cushing from Indiana, I believe it was, and I wanted to be her friend. I met her on Main Street and I knew she was new. This was in 1973. One evening I went out to her house in a trailer park, I knocked on her door. She came to the door and she told me that her husband said that she couldn't have anything to do with niggers. I didn't really understand what the word 'nigger' meant because growing up in Cushing, it was a small town and everybody got along with everybody. My white friends gave me lunch money when I didn't have it, I didn't see color. I wasn't taught that. I know today race is something that people instill in their children, because when you're young and innocent, you don't see color.

My second brush with race was when I worked for Gibble Oil Company in Cushing, Oklahoma. Mr. Gibble owned Gibble Oil and he had a daughter that worked there, a lady named Tennessee, and there were some other people. Things got bad so he wanted to lay off some help and I was the person that he laid off. Well, later on he came back to my house and asked me to come back to work. I think he realized they had done a discrimination thing against me. I cried because I really did like that job. I also used to work at the Cushing Hospital in Cushing. I was a nurse's aid and I truly enjoyed that because I liked helping people, giving to people. My son and my husband were so dedicated to loving me and my ex-husband always made sure that when I worked, that he took care of Maurice, our son, our only child.

Well, like most endings in a marriage, my marriage ended in a divorce. I left my husband, took Maurice and moved in with my mom in Tulsa. My husband threatened to take Maurice from me but I knew he loved Maurice as much as I did. Anyway, Maurice ended up with me.

After the divorce in 1978 I got ten thousand dollars. I took that money and opened up my first beauty salon and supply house in Tulsa, Oklahoma. I had two locations and did very well. I was very successful in 1979 and early 80's. I began doing fashion shows and called my business Maurice's Beauty Salon and Supplies and Maurice's Pretty Girls. In the year 1983-84, a company out of Duluth, Minnesota bought my company. They wanted to call it Maurice's that used to be in the State of Oklahoma. They liquidated the assets and moved away. When they moved away, they wanted to come back into the state. By that time I had formed a corporation under Maurice's, which was named after my son, Maurice Smith. So, I sold the name back to them, then I sold the equipment I had at the beauty salon to a different woman named Sirretta. Wow, we will talk about Sirretta later on in this story. I sold the company, then I became Pamela Smith's Enterprises, Pamela's Pretty Girls. I dropped Maurice after I sold it. I started doing fashion shows all around the world, started traveling, modeling clothes from different department stores, many, many stores. I became well known in the Tulsa area. This was in '82, '83 and '84. Very popular, Pamela's Pretty Girls. I booked concerts in the year 1985-86. The first show I booked was in the year 1986, I played Jay Blackfoot. Then I played Bobby Bland in Oklahoma City at the Lincoln Plaza. I was so new and green at it, I didn't even have a sound system and Bobby Bland said to me, "Pamela, what do you want me to do, go from table to table singing?" I started laughing because I didn't really understand about a sound system.

In 1986 I lost my grandfather, Ray Brannon. He was just like a dad to me because my mom and dad separated when I was a little girl of five. He walked off and left my mom with eight children, so my older brother and my sister struggled to make ends meet, to help mama raise the other sisters and brothers. My stepfather, James Pinkard died in '87. I lost my mother February 12, 1988. I was sitting down talking to my mom when she had a heart attack. It blew me away. I tried to revive my mother, I put her on the floor. I can remember to this day just screaming and hollering for help, running back and forth to the door.

After my mother passed in '88 I met a famous man named Willie Jones. When I met the singer, a friend of mine named Keith Turner, a promoter out of Dallas, had played him in Wichita, Kansas at the Cotillion Ballroom. When he played Willie Jones at the Cotillion Ballroom, I went up with him and a friend named Linda to book the show. Willie Jones liked me, saw something that he was interested in, and started making a pass. Well, to make a long story short, I got involved with Willie Jones in October of 1988. Yes, Willie Jones was married at the time. I was young, about thirty-three or thirty-four, still a young woman, I would say. I made a lot of mistakes, and this was the major mistake for me, the day that I allowed Willie Jones to enter into my world. I started dating Willie Jones, I was very vulnerable and hurting. My mother had died on February 12, 1988 and I met Willie Jones in October. I had it, going on until I met this man. A devil sent straight to me dressed in a leather suit in such a disguise. Let me tell you that's when my hell began. Nobody but God has been standing by my side through it all. Nobody but God.

In the year of 1989 I started doing drugs with Willie Jones. I never drank in my life, never smoked, still to this day don't drink and smoke, but I started using drugs. I got hooked on crack cocaine. My sisters had no clue that I was doing drugs because I'd always been a strong woman, always stayed away from vices like that, always could handle things. But I guess my mother's death had taken a toll on me more than I realized. I was my mother's baby. My mother was my everything, my best friend, my rock in time of storms and her death just devastated me to where I was so weak that when I did meet a man who was already involved in drugs and a slew of women, and being famous and him wanting me made me, it just impressed that a man that famous would fall in love with a country girl like Pamela. I lived in Tulsa but I still had a lot of country in me.

After I started using drugs, my sister Esther died, January 27, 1990. She died of an aneurysm. It broke my heart again. Here I'd lost my grandfather, my stepfather, my mother, and now my sister Esther, my second oldest sister. I had other sisters but it was just, the circle had been broken. And I knew then when the circle was broken, death was going to continue to knock on the Brannon's door. And it did. Nobody but God sustained me through all of this, all my downfalls, all my mountains, nobody but God. My niece Sheila, Esther's daughter, died in 1991 of Lupus, nineteen years of age. Well, I begged God not to let death knock on the Brannon's door anymore after Sheila died. I guess God hadn't gotten my attention. But death managed to continue to rise. I continued to get in trouble, still using checks and credit cards.

In May of 1993 I was in a hotel getting high with Willie Jones, doing drugs. People knew that drugs make you do some strange things. And in this hotel, I don't know what he was trying to do, but I know this man had been trying to harm me, hurt me for some reason. I really don't know what it was about. I guess the drugs just make you think somebody's out to get you paranoid. But anyway, to make a long story short, that night of doing drugs I'd been up three or four nights with him, he came to the hotel room, next thing I knew the police were knocking at my door, saying that they thought I had robbed somebody at the front desk, which was not so. What it was, I was in the hotel room with a fake name because Willie Jones was married. And by him being married, his wife would check up on him and check the hotels and follow him, so I was using an alias name. So when Willie Jones left the room that night some kind of altercation broke out at the front desk. I was up in my suite, the police knocked on the door and by me being in a hotel room with an alias name, I don't know, for some reason I had called them because I thought that this man, Willie, was trying to hurt me. I quit Willie a couple of times and got sick of abuse, the fighting, and the drugs and the life that he lived with all these different women. I just was tired of that and I was trying to get out of it, and I think for some reason he felt that. Anyway, the police came up and, by the grace of God, I don't know what it was, I told him that I had a brother that was in law enforcement and they asked me my birth date. I gave them 2-5 of '55. When they called my brother to verify the day of my birthday, they asked Leon Brannon, this Dallas police officer, could you verify your sister's birthday? My brother had no clue I was in a hotel in the midst of storms like that. He had warned me before to stay away from Willie Jones because he knew Willie was not liked, married and into drugs. My brother Leon gave them the date, February 5, 1955, but nobody but God, because I was on my way to jail that night because I was on parole down in Dallas, breaking the law in the hotel room at the Holiday Inn. Leon gave them that date and it just freaked me out. The officer let me go and told me what happened downstairs, that the reason why they thought that was because I was in a hotel using an alias name and they knew Willie Jones was mad and was trying to get me into some kind of trouble, set me up. I don't really know and I don't understand it to this day. To make a long story short, a friend picked me up from the hotel and I went to another friend's house.

CHAPTER 2

I was supposed to be in a wedding. My friend Linda was getting married in Oklahoma City. May 18, 1993 I was in jail in Garfield County. I had used some checks and credit cards and I turned myself in, and before I turned myself in, the judge and I got into it. I told the judge that day, before I was arrested, to go over there and turn myself in on the phone. I told him that I was sorry, that I'm not equal to him and his peers in this courtroom. He got angry with me and locked me up. My bond was one hundred thousand dollars. I sat in the Enid County Jail for close to a year until it was time I'd be sentenced. My family wanted to bond me out and I said no. It was my first time ever going to prison, my first time ever being in jail. But it was an experience for me. Nobody wants to be in jail, but I wasn't going to let my family spend one hundred thousand dollars to get me out of jail because I told the people in Garfield County why I was arrested for using illegal checks and credit cards. I didn't come to Garfield County to buy the county, I was just coming here to be arrested. So I sat there.

In December of 1993 I was sentenced to twenty years in Garfield County. For the twenty years I got I went on to Eddie Warrior Correction Center, Taft, Oklahoma (EWCC).

January 4, 1994 I was sent to EWCC for checks and credit cards. While in prison you learn a lot. I had no clue what it was like to be in prison. I was a lady that had everything going for her. I wasn't used to being locked up. I was used to telling people what to do, owning my own businesses, and jumping in my cars, jetsetting and going where I wanted to go. Then I found myself in a confined environment where somebody would tell me 'you'd better not cross the line'. Being in prison made me stronger, it helped me to sober up from my addiction, but I didn't learn enough about staying out of trouble in prison. I found out that being in prison with a drug addiction is not the answer, because if you don't get your addiction taken care of through some type of program, or some kind of high power, when you do get released you will find yourself a candidate back for prison. Well, I stayed in prison about fourteen months. In July of 1995 there was a program called SSP at EWCC. I made that program. That program was a hand-picked program by the Governor of Oklahoma. We had to have done so many days and your sentence couldn't be violent. Well I'm not a violent person. I was in for checks and credit cards, which landed me that lengthy sentence in the beginning.

July 14, 1995 I came home on SSP. I was so happy because I had a grandson that was born, named Kyante, that while I was in jail and didn't have an opportunity to see. By the way, they made a mistake and let me out of jail on the twenty year sentence and I went to Dallas and after I got to Dallas the bondsman came down and picked me up and put me back in jail, and that's where I stayed. Tulsa County made that mistake. I came home July 14, 1995. I was so happy, I got to see my sisters Diana and Elweeder. I had such a desire to stay out of prison because I knew that wasn't my life. But I had an addiction, I realized, that was stronger than I. I never thought that I would be a person that used drugs. I fell short.

Well, I met this man named Roy Brown in McAlester, Oklahoma. I had been in the treatment center in McAlester. That didn't work for me. My sister Diana Elweeder engineered a cooked-up scheme and Diana had me come to her house in Cushing late one night. I guess I would say this was probably about a year later. I didn't stay out long on SSP. I wasn't out long before my addiction landed me in trouble with checks and credit cards again. But this particular night Diana decided to have me come over to her house. She wanted me take a shower, get cleaned up, and she told me she wanted to take me for a drive. What she did, she took me to a rehab place in Stillwater, Oklahoma. When I went in the door locked. I knew then I'd been tricked. But I knew then and I know today, that my sisters Diana and Elweeder did that for nothing but love because they knew their little sister was so strong that there wasn't a mountain she couldn't climb, there wasn't a river she couldn't swim, and if anything was broken, Pamela could fix it. If she didn't fix it, she would still try. So they didn't like to see their little sister in that state of mind. It was taking a toll on them. They began to blame Willie Jones. Well, Willie Jones was a bad influence on me. I had choices, I just made bad choices. My addiction got stronger than I was. I stayed in the rehab in Stillwater for a couple of days. I called this guy named Roy Brown that I had married one night. I was dressed in some Daisy Duke shorts so high and he was in greasy work clothes. He was a mechanic in McAlester. We went to this preacher in McAlester and got married on June 25, 1996, I believe it was. When I got tired of being at the rehab in Stillwater I found a way to break out and I jumped over the fence. I went to a payphone and called Roy and Roy, I believe, wired me some money to a Western Union. I got a cab or a bus, I really can't remember how I got from Stillwater to Cushing, but it seemed like I hired a cab to bring me from Stillwater to Cushing, because he had sent me, it seemed like maybe a hundred dollars to get out of Stillwater and try to get back to Cushing to pick up my car, a Volvo, that he had bought me.

So after I broke out of this rehab in Stillwater I went to my sister Elweeder's house. Elweeder and my niece Missy were in the kitchen and they looked up and saw me walking through the front door. They couldn't believe what they saw. They were just devastated to see me. I told them I broke out and I wanted my car and I was heading to McAlester where my husband Roy was, a man that I was married to such a short time, a very short time. I got my Volvo and went down to McAlester. I hung out down there for awhile. I was mad and bitter at my sisters for what they had done to me, not knowing they did what they did because they loved me and I didn't understand it then, but I do today. Everything they did was simply out of love for me.

I stayed down in McAlester. This was in 1996, probably about July. When my drug addiction continued to be stronger, even in McAlester, I stayed away from them because of my addiction. After I had my addiction for so long, I came up to Tulsa to buy some drugs, and when I did I was so high that I remember calling my son and telling him because I didn't want anyone else to tell Maurice. I had begged my sisters not to tell him, I forbade them not to tell and hurt my son. I got sick and tired of being so high and not facing my demons. Whatever was drawing me to the drug abuse, which I know my drug addiction was greater than I, I know I can do all things through Christ Jesus who strengthens me. So I called my son and told him on the phone that his mother had been using drugs. My son could not believe it. He about had a heart attack, literally. His heart started hurting him, pounding very hard. Lisa, my daughter-in-law, told me that. I thought by telling my son that help would come my way, that my son was going to put his foot down and wasn't going to tolerate a lot of things that I was doing with my drug addiction. My sisters simply could not handle me because I was terribly spoiled and used to having my way. My son Maurice does not let me have my way. He's very stern, a good child, loves his mom and I love him equally. I thank God for my son and for the part he's played in my life today. After he found out I was using drugs, I thought it was okay now that he knows the secret's out, but it seems like my addiction got worse just because Maurice knew it.

When I was on drugs it hurt my family so much. But when you're on drugs you do some stupid things. I lied to Maurice, I lied to my friends, I lied to my family. Anybody who uses drugs knows there's no moral values in using drugs. You're a liar, you'll steal, you're a cheat. Yes I did that, and I regret it today, and I thank God for mending fences in my life with my family, that they loved me so much because they knew that wasn't me. They knew there was a chemical in Pamela that was not Pamela, and one day I would return.

My son took me to McAlester, Oklahoma and put me into rehab, The Oaks. I stayed in The Oaks for thirty days. After I came out of The Oaks, I did well for awhile, but not long. Shortly after that I found myself doing checks and credit cards again. August 10th of 1996 I went back to prison at EWCC, Taft, Oklahoma. I went to report to the probation lady and I told her that I had been in jail for some checks and some more things in McAlester. I turned myself in like always. I always pled guilty and I always turned myself in when I was guilty and knew I was wrong. The police didn't have to look for me. When I turned myself in to the probation lady, she took me to EWCC. I became a floor janitor, I worked hard because I wanted to get out of that place. I knew that this time I had to change, because I was going to lose everything I loved. And I knew change had to start within me and within the prison. That's where change had to start for Pamela. Not get out of prison and change, but change within – within myself and the prison cells.

I did well. I went to this case manager and I said 'If I do well, can I please leave here?' I realized then the light came on for me. Pamela, you've got to change. So I worked hard doing floors, I worked at the beauty shop for the gym supervisor and beauty shop lady. I went to this unit manager at EWCC and I asked if I could sign a pack. A pack is short for package that allows you, if you're not a violent crimer or low points, you can go up to lower security.

September of 1997 came. I had signed a pact and I was told to go to lower security. Lower security is at TCC in Tulsa, Oklahoma. TCC is Tulsa Correctional Community Center. I arrived at TCC in September of 1997. When I got to lower security I was so happy because there's a difference in higher security and lower security. You have more freedom at lower security, meaning that you don't have a fence around you, you can leave the site with permission to go to certain programs such as AA, church programs, different things like that, if you qualify. TCC lower security did not necessarily mean they could go off the grounds other than to work. I was only eligible to go off the grounds to work. I used to work for Wells Fargo in Tulsa, picking up trash, and that was in October. I got sick from high blood pressure and it kept me from bending over to pick up trash, so they pulled me off the Wells Fargo crew and brought me back in at TCC and reassigned me to Department of Public Safety (DPS), Jenks Northside. I became a trustee for DPS on 36th Street North. I started there in November of 1997. I had signed my paperwork to go to work for the DPS on 36th Street North.

When I signed the paperwork I was delayed a week because my sister Diana was killed in a car accident at 4:19 on November 9, 1997. It rocked my world. I lost it. I couldn't believe that my sister was killed and I was locked up. I couldn't grieve the way I wanted to grieve, being in a confined situation. You can't go hug the other grieving members of the family because you've got somebody dictating to you, you've got to get approval to go to this, or you may not get approval to go to that. But it was a devastating blow, so I was delayed a week, grieving at the center about Diana's death. I made preparations with the case manager to make preparations for my cousin Teanie Mitchell, who used to be in prison and had a prison ministry, to pick me up that Saturday and get me ready to go to my sister Diana's funeral. How sad was it that I got to see all my family members. I wasn't in chains but I knew that I had to remember what I promised myself, that I had to change within because I can't live like this. My family's hurting and my sister and my brothers are hurting to see their little sister having to go back to a prison cell and leave her family behind after the funeral was over. I hugged my brothers Leon, R.L. and Jimmy, and they even took up a collection to give me money to help me, and I fixed food from the funeral to take back. Just knowing that I had to leave my family and go back to strangers, rely upon my cellmate prison buddies for comfort, but knowing that I had God, who was going to send His comfort to me.

CHAPTER 3

The week after Diana's funeral I got myself together, ready to start to work that Monday in November of 1997 at DPS. I had gotten to work and called my brother Jimmy to let him know I was working at DPS on 36th Street North. He came up and brought some food to me and was happy to see me. I went in the break room and used the telephone. I knew that the rules were not to use the phone, not to have sex, not to have visitors, I knew all the PWP rules. But there was a man there, a State Drivers Examiner and a Supervisor. The Supervisor was over DPS Jenks and several other locations. Well the Supervisor was not there all the time, so when he wasn't there, he and the State Drivers Examiner were the two guys that went to Department of Corrections (DOC) rules about how to handle inmates, what they could do and what they could not do. So when the Supervisor wasn't around, the State Drivers Examiner was there to supervise inmates, which he did. He told us what to do. In fact, he told me what to do.

After my brother had left, the State Drivers Examiner told me that I broke the rules and I could get into trouble and be shipped to higher security. So I didn't think any more about it, but later on he told me I needed to do something to make him trust me. I had no clue what this man was talking about. I thought this man meant like, don't steal anything, don't get in any trouble, something to that effect. I had no clue that he was talking about what I ended up doing for this man to trust me. That was the most degrading thing of my life, the most sickening thing that I ever heard of. I was raped, forced, tortured and mistreated and abused in the hands of this State Drivers Examiner. After I realized what he was asking me, he asked me to show him my breasts. I went in the back storage room where most of my rape, in fact all of my rape, took place, a room where he would smoke and my janitorial supplies were kept. I lifted my blouse up to show him my boobs. He kind of stuck his head up like a snake and said something like 'God sure blessed you to have large breasts' or something, in that area with my breasts. But I knew then that when Jimmy came to see me, that when you're an inmate, they can make up anything on you and DOC believed it. They could say I stole a wallet and they could just be mad and DOC would believe what people say about an inmate. Yes, I know people go to prison to be corrected of their mistakes, but how would you ever be corrected when the state keeps that label of inmate and criminals attached to you. So I had to do what this man asked me to do because I wanted to see my family. My sister Diana just been killed and I wanted to bond with my family. My son Maurice would bring Kyante up and I would get to see them in the lobby, it was just different at lower security. It wasn't the same, it was a different freedom, just totally different. But I never left the site where anyone other than my three brothers, R.L., Leon and Jimmy, and two girlfriends, one named Sirretta and one named Brenda. With the exception of one time, a lady next door took me to buy some hot links.

Well, after I showed him my breasts, in December of 1997 I was in the back room engaged in oral sex, penetration sex, whatever you call it. This man knew that I broke the rules and he let me know what DOC could ship me back, and I could get myself a misconduct. I'd already been engaged in sex with him and I knew that he had something over me and I knew this was a state agency and these people weren't going to believe me. If I told them anything different they would just ship me back to EWCC and put me on lock down. When you're in prison, you go to lock if you tell somebody you've been raped. They send you straight to lock, like it's your fault. That's the part of punishment, to send the message to the other girls that if you cry rape, that is what you get, going to lock. And that's not the answer. Well, in December we had sex.

In January of 1998 this man, the State Drivers Examiner that raped me, forced me and threatened me, had told me that he had to go do a polygraph in Oklahoma City. He had to take a polygraph on a fifteen year old Afro-American girl that, in September of 1997, went up to the DPS on 36th Street North to obtain a written test. He said she flunked the test in September, took her in the back office, locked the door and made sexual comments to this young lady. The young lady came out of DPS and later on reported it to her teacher and her family, but he told me that he had to go to Oklahoma City to do this polygraph. When he came back he told me what the trooper said. The trooper said 'If you did this to my daughter, I would have hung you by your balls.' He told me he flunked the polygraph and they put a reprimand in his jacket for this little fifteen-year-old girl. I was thinking, this man is really sick, because you're guilty. Look what you've been doing to me. And I knew that nobody was going to help me if they've already overlooked this little fifteen year old girl's cry and said that the little girl was lying and made it up. I knew then, being an inmate, I didn't have a snowball's chance in hell for any help. I knew at that point nobody was going to believe me. This little girl was just an innocent civilian that came in with her grandmother to obtain a written test to get a drivers license. Well, in late January he asked me about a condom. He asked me to go next door and see if the guy who worked at a surplus store next door to DPS had a condom. This guy was one of his friends who he would watch dirty movies with. I went over there but I was kind of reluctant and shy and embarrassed to say that, so I came back and told the State Drivers Examiner that the guy didn't have a condom, so we went back over there together. When the Examiner realized that he didn't have a condom, he went up the street to a store that day but they were out, so the next day he came to work with a condom and gave it to me. I stuck it between two boards in the back storage room where I kept the supplies and where he hung out, smoking his cigarettes. One of his friends would come in the back and smoke. The others were allergic to smoke and didn't even go around smoke. So that left the State Drivers Examiner and me in the back storage room. After he gave me that condom in late January, I went and got it from those boards, walked into the office of a black drivers improvement guy and stuck it out in my hand and said 'Look what the State Drivers Examiner gave me.' He laughed in my face and said 'What you gonna do?' I said 'I'm gonna tell the Supervisor.' On February 6, 1998, for the rest of my life, I was raped on my birthday with that condom, threatened and reminded what he could do. He let me leave with girlfriends and go shopping, do certain things with Sirretta or Brenda.

After he raped me on my birthday that Friday, February 6, 1998, I went in the center and the girls at TCC had a party planned for me. They had all the food set up on a decorated ironing board, cake and chips and dip and pop, and all I could remember doing was running straight in and jumping in the shower, scrubbing and scrubbing and scrubbing, trying to scrub clean, and still found myself filthy. I just couldn't get clean enough, like I just wanted to scrub my skin outside my private parts. I was just so tired of the things that man had done to me, but for some reason my birthday has been ruined for the rest of my life. Every time I think of my birthday, I think of being raped on that day.

On February 18th I was riding in the state car with the Supervisor. I had told him about the man giving me a condom and going into the back storage room. He laughed and thought it was a joke. He even said he thought it was a joke. And I told him that this man was going to cause you all so much trouble one day.

A friend had received over twenty letters from girls saying they were raped and needed help but none of the girls had signed their names. And I understand that, because if you send a letter out with your name on it and help doesn't come, then you're going to suffer some kind of retaliation. They're going to put you on lock and then your story's out there but nobody has come to help or see about you. So I understand that, but every letter that I sent out of prison I signed. I was willing to stand, be prosecuted, be ridiculed, put on lock, I was ready at that point when I started sending those letters out for help. But after Sharon had told me that, we sat on her porch and she said, 'Pamela, I had a niece that went up there to that place to get her license, a written test. And, what's this man's name that violated you?' And I pointed to her on this piece of paper and she said, 'I think that's the same man that violated my niece.' And I said, 'What's your niece's name? Candace?' She said, 'Yes.' I just started jumping up, crying, shouting, because that morning I had asked God to order my footsteps, not knowing that my footsteps were going to carry me to this little child's house. I'd known of her story, the things she went through. I heard of her stories through court, how the people said in the trial that they never heard her side of the story, that the Supervisor got on the witness stand and testified that he spoke to the grandmother and the grandmother said she never met the Supervisor. Well, after I had cried and thanked God for all these seven years, not knowing who this fifteen year old girl was. I had no clue that I was going to meet her. I never knew who she was in all this time. I knew her name. Sharon told me that she lived right next door. I was so overwhelmed God ordered my footsteps that day, that I didn't even want to see Candace, I was still crying, knowing that God had just revealed Himself like that to me, and I was grateful for that. So I came home just shouting and telling some friends I ran into and I pulled them over and told them how God had ordered my footsteps that day, and I asked Him about Candace that day and I met her. He took me straight to her front door. So I just came home, just rejoicing.

A week passed by, I was really anxious to meet Candace, but I didn't want to push. So, I let another couple of weeks passed. My Petition was circulating in their church and her mother saw that Petition and saw that man's name and her mother said, 'Uh huh. I've been praying to God that this man gets caught up, and somebody else caught up with him' because she was thinking about what this man had done to her daughter. They signed the Petition. I went back that evening and met the grandmother that took Candace up to DPS to obtain her written test and witnessed her granddaughter coming out the back in a devastated state of mind, but didn't know what was going on. So I didn't meet Candace that day.

I finally met Candace. Beautiful, courageous, loving, young lady. She was sitting in her chair balled up, tall, slender, just a young version of Jane Kennedy. Just absolutely beautiful. I wasn't expecting that. I just wasn't expecting what I saw, I guess, I don't know. She's very smart, focused and told me that she admired me, that I'm her hero, that I had fought for her and that what this man, the State Drivers Examiner did to her, it just seemed like it was just happening to her at that moment, it was like it's still fresh in her mind. We cried, I cried a few tears after I sat there and just stared at her, just shocked after seven years to finally meet the young girl that I always said this man violated and should have been prosecuted for her. Coming face to face with her was like a dream come true. After that, we continued in bond that we were going to fight this thing together, and I told her that my fight is meant for her as well. To make a long story short, she did her first interview Friday, July 30th at the *Okie Claw*, a brave young lady. I had never really heard her whole story, and I wanted to go in the interview to hear it, and I wanted to be in there because I knew if her story was anything like mine, she was going to cry, and I wanted to cry with her, because I wanted to let her know it's okay to cry, because of what we both have gone through, it's okay to cry. How can you go through something like this without shedding tears? How can you go through something like this without being hostile and mad and angry? So I wanted to be in there with her, but the reporter told her mother and me that she was grown and she could do the interview on her own, so we accepted that. We went and sat in the lobby and the mother shared with me how the DPS people did them, trying to force Candace into doing a polygraph without her mother present. Her mother told them she was not going to do a polygraph at fifteen. They were loaded up and taken to some building that was not a polygraph facility and tried to get a statement out of Candace, which Candace did give a statement to the DPS and she gave a statement to the policeman at her school. For the first time her mom was telling me Candace's story.

When Candace came out the back it was just like a burden had been lifted off of her after seven years. So when she sat down to talk to me, the reporter took Candace's mother to the back. Candace sat there and told me her story for the first time. We sat there and she said, 'I told them that if they had prosecuted this man, Pamela wouldn't have gone through all this stuff, and I'm so sorry that you had to go through this Pamela.' And I told her, 'Don't worry about it.' I asked what type of questions they asked her and she said 'Just, you know.' She said that she started crying, and I told her it was okay to cry. 'How could you go through something and not cry? It's okay, Candace, you can cry. But one thing about today, you finally got to tell your story. You got to tell your story, your side of it. They can't continue to say you were a spoiled brat and make this up on the State Drivers Examiner.'

CHAPTER 4

Let me tell you about the press. I've been begging the press for seven years, Channel 2, Channel 6, Channel 8, to do my story. I sent Channel 6 a story while I was in prison back in 1998. It never got told. I was told that they tried to contact the prison but the prison wouldn't let inmates do stories. And when we did do stories in prison, we were dictated on what to say and if we said anything other than what we were told to say, we'd get a misconduct and probably go to lock. So we were always threatened if we talked to staff when they came on the ground, all types of things. Anyway, after Channel 6 didn't come and do my story, I continued to write letters, begging press to come. Since I've been home, and since I've been through trial January the 6th through the 13th, the next day after my trial was over, I went to the Tulsa newspaper and did an interview, a two and a half our interview. That story yet has not been published in the paper. I have a copy of that interview. I sent Channel 2, Channel 6 and Channel 8 documents. I made the video for the Governor of Oklahoma, sent it to them. It has not been on the television yet. I have spoken out in so many churches on this case when my petition drive was going, asking the community to help me. I spoke at Friendship Baptist Church on July 4th, with a standing ovation. Channel 81's Rosie Tott came out and filmed me speaking at Friendship Baptist Church, Reverend Wendell Tisdale. When I finished speaking it was a standing ovation. Rosie said she wanted people to come out and see what the public expression was when I would tell them that I was raped. First of all, my community didn't know anything about this case. All they knew was what I told people, because I know so many people. It's not that the press would tell this story. It's not that this case is not one-hundred percent true. Anytime a woman wants to go on television and tell a story so degrading, it's got to be nothing but true, because first of all, they say that women are too shameful. Yes, it's a very shameful story, but I'm not going to be that eighty percent of women that are ashamed to report or talk about it. And I'm not going to be that other twenty percent that once you do have a chance, you get scared and intimidated, worried about what your friends and family say. I'm going forward. After Channel 81 sent the men out to do it and I got a copy of it, I believe in my heart that Channel 81 did that interview to give it to the State of Oklahoma. I believe that in my heart and I will tell you why later.

I contacted Rosie and told her that the man came out and taped it, so on July 10th or 11th of 2004, she had an appointment for me to show up that morning to do an interview for Channel 23 here in Tulsa. Jabar Shumate, the young gentleman that's running for State Representative went with me. We got in the studio and Rosie Tott said, 'I have been contacting DOC and can't get any report.' I said, 'Well it's not DOC you need to be contacting. You should be contacting the Attorney General's office.' So she jumped up and ran out of the room to go try to get a statement from them. She came back and said, 'Well I can't tell this story because if the State of Oklahoma won't give their side, we can't tell your side, because that's not fair to them.' Well I said, 'Well that's not fair to me' Jabar Shumate said, 'That's not fair to Pamela. If the State doesn't want to talk, why won't you tell this story? Why don't you tell this story? That's not fair. If she wants to tell it and they refuse to give a comment, that shouldn't hold up Pamela talking.' 'I know, but we don't want to be sued. We need both sides of the story.' The only reason why they didn't tell this story is simply because the State of Oklahoma has somewhere told these people 'don't tell her story'. First of all, if this story was ever to be told, published on television, don't you know that the State of Oklahoma would be in an outcry, that people would panic for their wives and daughters to go to the drivers' examiner's place? This man, I remind you, quit his job after fourteen years. He flunked the fifteen year old girl's polygraph, refused to do one for me and resigned his job the day he was supposed to do a polygraph. Now Channel 81 declined to do the story. Now what it was, the reporter, a black, young, aggressive lady, was excited about doing it. But her boss then told her, 'You can't do that story' just because I was going against the State. That's the only reason. She couldn't say that. We walked out of the studio together, she and I, the cameraman and my friend and she told us she was going to go by a fast food restaurant where the men were sitting there everyday, collecting signatures. Rosie Tott and this cameraman showed up and the only reason she showed up, I believe, was just to try to make me think that she was sincere because she said, 'I don't want my community to think that I don't want to tell this story, and I don't want them looking down on me.' 'Well, that's okay' I said, 'don't worry about it. I realize being in a white man's world that they run everything and simply because you're just an employee, you're not running anything.' I said, 'Can I have a copy of that tape that you taped of me?' She said, 'Yeah.' I said, 'The one you filmed at Friendship?' She went looking for the tape. She said, 'I can't find that tape.' I said, 'You know why you can't find it? Because somebody gave it to the State of Oklahoma to see what I had to say, to see what type of reaction my community has. They won't put it on television.' She said, 'Oh no, they can't do that.' Rosie Tott's got a lot to learn. She's young, she's new and she's kind of green when it comes to threat, and certainly green when it comes to the State of Oklahoma, how dirty they are. The State of Oklahoma misuses black folks so bad. Anytime a woman can be raped and it's okay to let a man quit his job and think that it's okay and to torture a black woman – a woman, period. And then not put it on the news, pick and choose the news, I feel like my community was robbed of this case simply because they have a DPS headquarters sitting in the heart of north Tulsa. Our people should have been informed of this case, but the television stations would not air it, simply because the State probably told them that if you air bad things about us, when we get some good news we won't give it to you. It's not about suing and liable. How do you win all the way in District Court and make it to Federal Court and get law books if your case is based on a lie. That's just what the State of Oklahoma is afraid of. Not one time have these people come and said that we're going to lock you up for perjury. We're going to do this to you or do that to you. Haven't any of those people come because, you know why? They want Pamela Smith to go away. I don't know why the State Attorney General's office wants to come on the television with the State Drivers Examiner, that he has to have an attorney and won't talk. I don't understand why they want to go on the television and say that she's lying or say anything different. What I'm saying, I don't need videos. I can't get the television to tell the story, they won't do an interview with me. I have <u>begged</u> the press, <u>begged</u> the press to come sit down and do an interview of me. Now, Candace and I will join up together in doing everything we can. We're going to put her story out, we'll go stand in line at a fast food restaurant, we're going to pass this story out so everybody knows about this man in the State of Oklahoma. The State of Oklahoma knew this man was guilty and they figured, get rid of him, it was about saving money to them. It wasn't about justice. It was not about justice. So where we're at today is, just right now, continue to press forward and hope that some press will come along with this story. This shouldn't have taken me to get out and knock on doors and go out to get a Grand Jury. But that's the only way I could get help. I didn't trust the State. How's the State going to prosecute the man that worked for the State and raped me and tortured me and forced me, raped me with a glass salt shaker and wanted to insert a pencil in me. But I'm just believing in God. Everything that I've done up until this point, I will continue to seek God and trust God. I know God will prevail for me. I know that every door that ever slams in my face, God just opened up a window and I'd just jump through the windows. They can't slam doors in my face and think that I'm shut down, because if there's a door shut, God will open up a window. And I know that. So I will continue to fight this case and move forward.

CHAPTER 5

Today is Monday, August 2, 2004. I will continue to tell my story as this case progresses. So many people came together, so many rape victims came out of this. One was raped by her stepfather and she said, every night when she'd go to bed she tried to figure out how to kill the man, burn him up or kill him in some type of way without everybody knowing she did it. She said she went to her mother to tell her mother she was raped but her mother didn't believe her. I've heard women come tell me that as a child they were raped by their own loved ones. I had a young lady come here and tell me that the neighbor man raped her little sister, three years of age. A lady that helped me on the petition, faithfully, every Saturday and Sunday at the flea market, had three daughters. Three daughters. And I think the oldest one today may be twelve or thirteen. And these girls were raped, all three of them, the same day by the man across the street. So, God is allowing me to do a lot of good things with this case. I will speak out, I will do a lot. I will not, I will not sit down and have the devil have his way on this case. I will allow God to continue to move mountains and give me strength to do the things that I need to do. I did talk to Candace today. I asked her about a police report and she said she did make a police report. When she was at Central High School the black officer did the police report. She called and gave me a copy of the police report number. I got a copy of the police report number when she made this report on September 18, 1997. She was going to Central High School. I do have a copy of her story and her statement, what she did do about this case and where she was going with it. I will pick up on this on August 3, 2004.

November 2002. This is a significant number to me because I know it belongs to God, and I know I belong to

God. My husband Eddie was standing at a jukebox trying to play some blues and I said, 'Do you mind if I play my music first? Because I just have two dollars and you're going to be here all night with this five dollar bill.' He said, 'Well, why don't we play it together?' And we played some music together, then we got ready to dance. I asked him to dance and he told me he was a truck driver and he was just home off the road and stopped in there to have him a drink because he'd been on the road driving his truck. And we danced and I asked him about his cell phone. I had a Sprint phone and he had a Sprint phone. And I said, 'Well your phone looks like mine' and he said, 'Oh, this is a business phone, nobody gets my number.' So I didn't ask for the number, he was just rattling it off. When it got time for us to leave, my nieces and nephews and all were getting ready to leave because it was getting late, about eleven thirty or twelve o'clock that night, and I was getting sleepy anyway, and so I said, 'Walk me out to my car.' When he got to the tail end of the car he gave me his number and started rattling off the number and I thought to myself, this was a business phone and nobody got this number. So we exchanged numbers and I went on the road with him the next day, to Kansas, I believe, and ever since then we have been together. My husband told me, 'I'm going to give you my Social Security number, buy us a home.' He gave me his Social Security number the second day we were together and I could not believe it. I said, 'God, this has got to be my husband. No man gives you their Social Security number and says 'go buy us a home'. What little bit I didn't know, my husband was all messed up in a previous relationship and was still married. When he came to Tulsa to stay with me, I was so wrapped up in God. I promised God that I didn't want any more married men, I don't want my life messed up, I wanted to live for Him. Well when Eddie moved in with me I couldn't even sleep at night. I would cry and Eddie would tell me, 'Pamela, I will move back to the city because I don't want to come between you and God' and I told him, 'No, we need to get married.' We got married, had a beautiful church wedding. God gave me a wonderful man, a sweet man, a man that I knew loved me. Out of all the men I ever had in my life, I knew this man loved me, and that's a good feeling. My husband has been standing by my side ever since.

I did a deposition on this case back in 2001, I believe. And when I did the deposition at the attorney's office, the Supervisor was there. It was very heartbreaking for me to see this man because I couldn't believe that a man that I respected, that didn't judge me and didn't treat me like an inmate, we couldn't even speak to each other. My lawyers told me 'Don't say anything to him, just, if he speaks, it's okay to speak back, but don't talk to him' and I didn't say anything. I made it through the deposition that day. It was very painful but we got through it. They did a deposition on the State Drivers Examiner the next day. My lawyers felt like he was the biggest liar there was. My lawyer saw the Supervisor and the attorney for the State Drivers Examiner down in the lobby and he said they didn't know who he was. He came upstairs and said, 'I don't know what you all did to those lawyers, but they're down there scratching their heads.' The fact that they were on a fishing expedition because the State Drivers Examiner would not tell these people what I was saying. Had he told these people everything that I knew, and it would let them know he raped me. So what he had to do was keep denying everything. A person could not make up all of this. It'd take you fifty years to create a story like this – places, people, events and things. Anyway, he came upstairs and told us, 'You all kick butt or something because those people downstairs are scratching their heads. They don't know which way to go.' After that deposition was over with, May of 2001, we got ready to go to trial. But I want you to know, all along I had been writing letters to Channel 6, <u>begging</u> them to help me tell this story, get it out of the prison gates so we can get some of this rape to stop in the prison system on these girls and people hear their cries and these men can be prosecuted. The press ignored my cry. I wrote Oprah Winfrey while I was in prison. I wrote Jesse Jackson, I wrote Kenneth Copeland, I wrote T. D. Jakes, I wrote everybody you can imagine. I wrote Senator Maxine Horner. Senator Maxine Horner answered my cry. She stood by my side then and she's still standing by my side. She has followed up on my case and done everything she possibly could to help me. Maxine is like a big sister to me and I know she believes in me. She is called the Prison Mom.

In May of 2001 we got ready to go to Federal Court. I won at every level, District Court, Federal Court. At the time we were having these motions filed the Judge was steadily ruling in my favor. At the Federal Courtroom we got ready to go to trial that day, prepared. We were ready to go. At that time a lady was the State Drivers Examiner's attorney. She's the one that did the deposition on me at my attorney's office. We got ready to go to trial that day. The Judge called my attorney, her associate and the Examiner's attorney back into his chambers. My attorney told the Judge that the Attorney General's office had been threatening three ladies from EWCC. One's name was Katie McClain. If they show up to testify at this case, their jobs will be threatened. So Liz told the Judge that and the Judge told the Attorney General to go back and tell the Attorney General's office and anybody else he will hold them personally responsible if anybody else threatened these ladies as of today. We were going to court for trial, so they showed up to try to get Summary Judgement on the State Drivers Examiner. He wanted Summary Judgement to keep from going to prison. Well, the Judge denied him qualified immunity. The day we were going to trial, May 7, 2001, the State appealed the Judge's ruling, sent it Denver. It sat at Denver for a year and a half. My attorney and her attorneys in the State of Oklahoma had to go to Denver for oral argument on the 8th Amendment, Cruel and Unusual Punishment to establish that just because you're not a prison guard, it doesn't mean you can rape an inmate and get by with it. And that's what the State was simply trying to establish, that the State Drivers Examiner was not a prison guard, he was a state worker, so he should be shielded. The Judge said no, the case went to Denver at the 10th Circuit

Court of Appeal in Denver and it sat there for a year and a half. August 12th the Judge's ruling was upheld. They established a law in my name, Pamela Smith, Cruel and Unusual Punishment. I have a ruling in my name in the law books in Denver on the Cruel and Unusual Punishment, the 8th Amendment. After the ruling came down in September from the 10th Circuit Court of Appeal, we were prepared to go to trial again, Judge Combs' court.

I lost a brother, Leon Brannon, the Dallas police officer, in 2002 to a massive heart attack. That rocked my world, crumbled my world. I didn't know what to think. After that happened to Leon, I went to Dallas, a beautiful service with the Dallas police office for sixteen years. All I could think was, my brother that gave me all the words and encouragement, fight sister, fight, don't give up, keep fighting, keep fighting. Don't let these people do you like that. And I remember everything my brother said and I continue to fight. Continue to fight. Although battles look like they were about won and the victory was slipping away from me, I still remember what God told me the promise was. I know the promise I made to God and I know His promise to me. And I could hear my brother Leon saying, 'Fight, sister, fight. Don't give up. Whatever you do, don't give up.'

In December of 2003 my lawyer and another attorney called me to her office and said, 'We got a settlement offer. Can you be here?' I had my grandson with me and I was taking him to the doctor. I took my brother R.L. with me, my older brother, Ray Brannon that we call R.L. He's the oldest and he's been a faithful brother, a good brother, helped bury half his family, been good to everybody in his family, and still standing by his little sister's side, making sure that little sister doesn't get anymore wrongfully done to her. Even from a financial standpoint he's wanting to see this thing through.

We went to Liz's office. She sat there and in front of my brother told me there was a sixty thousand dollar offer. I told her she was crazy, I didn't want any sixty thousand dollars, I'm going to court all the way. This isn't about money. I want this man to go to jail. I want them to suffer and be embarrassed, like this man has done me. This man needs to pay. She said, 'Well Pamela, you're taking a chance.' I was so upset with my attorney because I couldn't understand how you take a million dollar case and reduce it down to sixty thousand dollars, when all along I didn't care about any money. If it was about money, I would have taken the sixty thousand dollars but it wasn't. This was about taking this man to court, embarrassing this man, degrading this man the way he did me. And it hurt me, misused me, and the State needs to be responsible for this man, not let this man resign, thinking that he could resign his post and relinquish them from liabilities of this man's actions and what he did to me. So after that I told her no I went home, very upset with my attorneys.

The next day Robert Martin, one of Liz's associates called me. My brother was here at the house with me. It was during the holidays. 'Why are you doing us like this?' he asked. I said, 'I'm not doing you all like anything. I'm just simply not going to take any sixty thousand dollars. We're real close to going to trial and I'm not going to settle this case. I want to go to trial. I don't care if I don't win any money, I want to embarrass the State like they have embarrassed me and let the public know what they've done to me. This is painful to me. This isn't about money.' Well, to make a long story short, they were simply trying to get out of work. I was informed later that they were trying to go on a skiing trip and they didn't want to work because the trial was set for January the 6th, and that means that right after Christmas, they couldn't get their party on to do what they wanted to do and be ready for trial January the 6th of 2004. I didn't settle for the money. They said the insurance company wanted to settle tonight, and if you don't take this money tonight, it won't last. I said, 'Well that doesn't make sense to me. I'm not going to take this money. What's going to happen? Is the money going to spoil or something if I don't take it tonight? I'm not going to take this money.'

January 6th I stood my ground. I was upset with the attorneys for trying to force me to take some money to trix my case off simply because I had been informed my attorney is kind of lazy and she likes to grandstand and she has trixed off a lot of cases. This is what Robert Martin has told me. Since he has been removed from her law firm, he said that they sometimes couldn't pay their bills and he would call up clients and settle the case for a little or nothing to pay their bills. And I said, 'Well, I'm not going to settle my case for anything other than going to court. If I walk out of there with an empty judgement, at least I will have gone all the way.' And that's what it was about to me was justice. All I've ever looked for in this case was true justice. That's all. True justice, not blind justice, not colored justice, not anything but true justice. So if I didn't take that, we ended up in trial.

Now let me tell you about a trial from hell. A trial from hell. January 6th through January 13th, 2004, my case was a 42 U.S.C. 1983 Civil Rights case. They picked the jury. When they picked the jury, it was an all white jury. There was a black lady sitting out there, but the State did not pick this black lady to go on the stand. I had eight jurors. Eight, I believe it was four women and four men. They all were white. I said to my lawyer after the jury was picked, 'I guess it's not bad having an all white jury. They're more abreast about rape than my race of people.' So I thought that would be a good thing. What little bit did I know, I didn't realize that I had a racist jury sitting in front of me. If they made that movie *Runaway Jury*, it defiantly set the tone for Pamela Smith in this case. I know Tulsa, Oklahoma has black folks. There was a black lady sitting there in the jurors, they could have picked her and put her on the jury. But no, that would have meant that I would have had a hung jury, and they weren't going to have that. Well, they picked the jurors. I got on the stand and I gave my testimony. I testified how this man shoved the glass salt shaker up my vagina, covered with plastic, wanted to insert a pencil up me, how he took me to the park, how my sister was dying in the hospital, how this man would threaten me, repeatedly rape me, how he gave me a condom, took the condom and showed it to the drivers improvement guy, how I told the Supervisor. I told the jurors all of this. Every bit of this. I cried my heart out. I cried. I've been crying, crying, crying. But yet, remind you, a case this powerful, the worst rape case on an inmate in Oklahoma history, has never, ever had the story told. They would not tell this story simply because the State knows this man is guilty. They know Pamela Smith knows that I know the State knows this man is guilty. And they have done everything to keep this story out of the press. They should have told this story when this man violated the little fifteen year old girl that went over to DPS on September 18, 1997 to get her written test. Had the State done something to him for this little fifteen year old girl, Candace Rowe, they would have not been hearing from Pamela Smith today if they had done something about him. But they didn't believe her.

A doctor, Steve Hoyer, who saw me at Eddie Warrior for about eleven months, got on the stand and testified that this was the worst rape case he had ever seen, that I suffered post-traumatic stress disorder. I didn't even know that I suffered that. You see how good God is? He took care of me, even knowing that I was suffering some emotional trauma, and not knowing that I had post-traumatic stress disorder until I got to trial in January of 2004, when the doctor testified on the stand. A DOC worker got on the stand and testified that my behavior was not the same as the happy, lucky person Pamela Smith was. Another DOC worker testified that she's the first person reported it during the trial. Yet another DOC worker testified that I worked in the gym and I wasn't the outgoing person I was before. Sirretta got on the stand and testified that this man took us to the park, hugging Sirretta. The jury refused to hear that. They simply refused to hear my side of the story, this all white jury made up in their minds that they were not going to believe Pamela Smith. The State told the jurors 'I'm going to prove she's a con.' In the courtroom they called me everything but a child of God. They called me a con, going to prove that I was the biggest con there is, which has nothing to do with rape.

Nothing to do with rape. I knew going into court with a conviction, a past record and being black, that I was going to be scandalized, but I never dreamed that a jury would hear how a woman was tortured so bad with a glass salt shaker, that they could not overlook my eleven year old conviction and my skin color and find this man guilty, instead of letting this man walk out of a civil trial with all the damage this man has imposed and inflicted upon me. There are other victims this man violated. There are other women that I know about.

There was a young lady named Jancies Strong that he told me that he had her show her private parts to him in the DPS storage room on 36th Street North before I worked there. I went back to the center and asked this young lady if that was true. She told me that yes, it was true. They used this young lady during trial and she was so drug related on the stand it was unreal. The State asked her, did I call her and tell her to lie for me? She said, 'Yes' under oath on the stand. First of all, I'd like to say this. That young lady was a lesbian in prison. I didn't fool with that kind of 'stuff'. I was in prison to change my mistakes, mend the fences that I broke down and build some bridges and get on with my life. I wasn't thinking about Jancies Strong, she was not my kind of friend in prison. So she got on the stand and lied. The State Driver Examiner wrote a letter to the Parole Board to get her out of prison, so she told the State. He helped her come home so the Attorney General's office used her on the stand. A payback to the State of Oklahoma.

The State called the State Drivers Examiner's wife to the stand and my attorney cross-examined her. My attorney came over to my table, leaned down with both hands on the desk, looked me dead right in my eyes and said, 'Do I attack her?' I said 'Yes. Jump in with both feet' because I saw what this courtroom of DPS employees was doing, coming in, jumping on the stand, making up lies and anything they felt big enough to say that would discredit me or make me look bad, far from the case itself that I was raped, tortured and forced with a glass salt shaker, instrumentation, that this man was sick, he was a predator, that he had done things to other women and the State just turned a deaf ear to it. A man doesn't quit his job after fourteen years. Do you remodel a building over three times? Change policy and procedure if a person's not guilty? This man quit his job, refused to do a polygraph simply because he knew he was guilty. She went back to the podium and said, 'Ma'am, I don't believe we met before. I'm the attorney for Pamela Smith. Ma'am, what type of underwear does your husband wear? Does he wear the Fruit of the Loom with the little lines?' The two Assistant Attorney Generals jumped up shouting, 'Objection, Your Honor!' and the Judge said, 'What did you say? What did you say Counsel?' So she said, 'Your Honor, I asked the defendant's wife what type of underwear her husband wore.' And he said, 'Go ahead, go ahead.' He allowed Liz to proceed with her questions. These new Attorney General's assistant had only been on the case three weeks, came in and used my past and my skin color to tarnish a jury instead of the facts of this case. They bragged they robbed me of a verdict, but they haven't. Also, my attorney asked the State Drivers Examiner's wife about his very close veins in his leg. That pissed the State off, so when the wife's little feelings were wounded, my attorney told the First Assistant Attorney General way before these two young, inexperienced girls took on this case, came in and robbed my attorney of a verdict that she had been working on this case for seven years. Robbed her of a verdict and said to the jury that I was a con and don't believe anything I say and looking at an all white jury opposed to a black woman, it just wasn't flying in that courtroom for me. No justice was going to be granted in Pamela Smith's honor. Not with an all white jury. So, when my attorney attacked the wife, because I knew that the State Drivers Examiner only made his wife a witness so that she could not sit in the courtroom and witness the things that were going to be said about her husband, so making her a witness would keep her out of the courtroom. Well, that's why he did that. My attorney told the First Assistant Attorney General back on May 7, 2001, 'You should not put his wife on the stand. My client is already a victim, don't make his wife a victim.' But that's what he wanted, and that was selfish on his part to show just how selfish and how sick-minded and twisted this man is. After my attorney attacked her with facts, that I knew the type of underwear, after giving this man oral sex and doing all the things that I had to do to this man to continue to see my loved ones and keep from being shipped back to higher security, that I knew where this man's close veins were and I knew also what type of underwear this man wore.

Also, when the time came for a DPS employee to get on the stand, this is still during the trial of 2004, but back early on at the DPS days like in 1998, the DPS employee gave me a Christian book, and in this book she signed it and said, 'Dear Pamela, You are a true servant of God that your work would never go unnoticed. Keep up the good work. Jesus is looking for good people like you to be good servants' or something to that effect. I found that page just before we went to trial, I saved that book because it was a nice Christian book, and I tore the cover off and gave it to my attorney who said, 'When I call her on the stand I'll see what she'll have to say about you.' Well when she called her up on the stand, she said to her, 'Ma'am, I'm the attorney for Pamela Smith. I know we never met before' and the employee said, 'No.' my attorney said, 'So you think Pamela is a servant of God?' 'No, I don't think that, no' the employee answered. My attorney said, 'You don't think she's a servant of God, a true servant of God?' 'No. She was a good housekeeper, that's what she was good in.' My attorney said, 'Well ma'am, let me show you something' and she took it up to the podium for her to read and said, 'Ma'am, read that.' 'It says, Dear Pamela, you are a true servant of God. Your work will not go unnoticed. Keep up the good work,' or something to that effect, and 'God is looking for true servants.' My attorney said, 'Now what did that mean?' She said, 'Well I meant that she was a good housekeeper.' My attorney said, 'But you were referring to Jesus.' She said, 'Yeah, but not for her.' 'Since when has Jesus been a housekeeper?' my attorney asked. The lady's face got so red, she got so mad, so bent out of shape, she said, 'Well Pamela Smith bragged on how she swindled old people out of cash money, out of five thousand dollars.' Not true! That is so far from the truth. I used credit cards, I did use a lady's credit card. Most of the credit cards I used were without permission from anybody. Otherwise, if there was permission, they wouldn't have been stolen. I never bragged on anything I've ever done, even in my addiction I knew right from wrong, but my addiction was too strong, but I never, ever, in a sober mind, would brag to a policeman, a woman whose husband is a trooper with the Oklahoma Highway Patrol (OHP), would I sit up and brag to her that I swindle old people out of money? Now, the credit card that I used, the particular person she's talking about was an old lady that lived in the apartments where I lived. I never told her that. They even looked in my jacket and saw what my crime was, I never swindled that lady out of anything. I'm not proud of the things I did. There never was any cash, it was nothing like that. But the fact of what it was, during the trial, if my attorney could throw a punch and knock the wife blindsided, they had to send somebody in that was evil enough and just prejudice enough to get on the stand and lie and say that. These people from DPS were supposed to be Christian, Bible packing people. They had Bible studies in Jenks. They had Bible studies on the North Side, but you couldn't tell it the way DPS lied on that stand against a poor little, former ex-inmate, convict, old crack head that I was, but yet a child of God. They had to come in and bring the whole DPS employment to get on the stand as character witnesses for the State Drivers Examiner. Now, during this trial, my attorney asked about four or five of his friends, and especially this employee, 'the State Drivers Examiner is your friend?' 'Yes.' 'Do you all go to church together?' 'No.' 'Do you and your husband and the wife all go bowling?' 'No.' 'Well what do you all do together besides work?' 'Nothing.' 'And you call that a friend?' This is how this story continued to go. It never, ever was anything other than built on a bunch of lies that DPS was told to come in, no matter what it took, they needed to prove that I was a liar, and no matter what they had to say under oath, just do it to keep Pamela Smith from getting this judgement. Now, I was raped, I was tortured, I was forced. I do believe that the State of Oklahoma has fooled the public and the jurors but they didn't fool me. I know they know this man is guilty, but if you can come to court and tarnish one's past, make a ruling in 1996, the State, it's a crime to have sex with an inmate. If you're going to have a ruling to say that, why would you allow inmates come to court, to make a petition be known if you're going to use our past and our skin colors? This eleven year old conviction to come into court to try to win a conviction? It wasn't enough to stop me. I will not stop. I will continue to press forward.

The State Drivers Examiner got on the stand. My attorney asked the State Drivers Examiner during the trial about the little fifteen year old girl that he took in the back room, that she went to do a written test with her grandmother, and when she went to do the written test, he said she flunked it, and he took her in the back, locked the door and asked her for sex. Now, I would like to say, my attorney asked the State Drivers Examiner on the stand, under oath, 'Why did you take that young lady to a back room?' He said, 'She had a bad attitude.' She asked him 'Well who gave you authority to chastise somebody's child or the client that comes through the door?' It was just a lie, he was guilty, he knows he's guilty, and he was planning on raping that little fifteen year old girl.

I had met another lady that told me a story about this man, and the story that she told me lines right up with Candace Rowe's story. This woman went in to do a CDL seven times and flunked her test and he took her in the back and suggested sex to her. The State of Oklahoma thinks that they got away with not paying damages, and if this is the message they send, that it's okay to rape a woman, and we can just let him quit his job. I know one thing, God is going to let this case come back to haunt the State really bad one day. I have to stand on God's promises, I will stand on God's promises and what He promised me – justice. I know sometimes it looked kind of dim for me. The battles looked like they were all won and it was all over. But I would not count God out. And even when I get devastating blows, God says 'Stand' and He said 'Count it all joy.' I am a faith believer. I stand on the word, I stand on God, His promises, and no matter how high the creek rises, I will still swim to shore because I know God is guiding me and He will be there for me. He's always been there. I have endured a lot in my life and I will continue to endure things and I know God called me to do this. This wasn't anything that I set out to do. But I know that by me standing up, coming out, informing women that you don't have to be quiet and hide and be ashamed when somebody robs you and violates your body. You have to stand strong, but you first have to trust God when you're taking a battle on. I never let the Attorney General's office, the District Attorney's office, the OHP, DOC, I never let any of those big names intimidate me. I know that my name, being a child of God, is the greatest name of all. I am the king's daughter. I'm heir to everything that God owns. And first of all, I first have to know who orders my footsteps and my footsteps are ordered by the Lord. I would like to say that after all these DPS people got on the stand and testified and lied, one employee got on the stand just to lie that I did a table dance or I rubbed my breasts on him. First of all, everybody that knows me, and I'm a well known woman, knows that's not true. First of all, I don't really know how to dance. The only dance I can do, and I do it okay, is the Electric Slide. But that was just to suggest that I was a happy person in a state of mind. You can't be happy when somebody's torturing you and raping you. You don't ever forget that. This is what the black officer that I took and showed the condom to in late January in his office, stuck it out in my hand, he testified on the stand to the jurors that I brought a condom in his office and showed it to him. Now where was that help? This jury was just doomed to not believe a black woman over a white man. Anytime you've got four white women sitting on a jury and you hear a woman that's been raped and tortured so badly, you know they'd have to be prejudiced and racist because if I was sitting on a jury and I heard that as a woman, I could feel that woman's pain. I even saw one of the lady jurors when I was on the witness stand crying while I was telling about the glass salt shaker. But in the closing remarks an attorney told the jurors to look at him and look at her. If that's not racist remarks I don't know what is. This case has been built on a cover up, a bunch of lies from DOC, DPS, District Attorney's office. There is not even a police report on my case. There's never been a police report. I brought in a Grand Jury to investigate this case, hoping to get a Grand Jury. It's been a struggle. It's been a struggle, struggle, struggle. But DOC didn't call the Tulsa Police Department, DPS didn't call and neither did the District Attorney. Now when this trial was nearing the end, the Judge told the jurors, 'Now if you don't want to come back tomorrow, you hurry up and get a verdict in.' Well that kind of meant to me, make them rush. They came back in fifteen minutes. A trial that took seven years of hell. It took seven years of torture of this case, it took seven days of trial and it took a jury fifteen minutes to go run in the back, after hearing all this strong evidence. But I guess it's hard for an all white jury to look at a white man and then look at a black woman and the Assistant Attorney General that had been on the case just three weeks, tell them that if I could sell a fish water and don't drink the water, it would be poison. All the things that these people said about me, it didn't hurt me, it just made me stronger, because I know who I am in God. I have faith. I have cried so many tears, but these tears, every one of them I know God has bottled up and put them in a bottle, saving them for me. And I know that God is going to make every one of these people answer to these lies that they told. I sent word for the Attorney General to call me. I got on the air and I called the District Attorney to get in contact with me. That has not happened.

After this trial was over, they came back in fifteen minutes and rendered a verdict to this man, the State Drivers

Examiner. I was devastated. I was blown away. There's just no way. A doctor testified... They had no professional witnesses, just DPS employees saying anything they wanted to say on the stand.

After the trial was over with, I couldn't believe it. My husband and I walked out of the courtroom in disbelief. I came home. I couldn't sleep. I walked around the house in a state of mind like I was about ready for a nervous breakdown. I could not believe what had just happened to me, after a week of testimony, two days on the stand of crying my heart out, I just couldn't stop the tears, just so thankful to God that I could cry after seven years, thinking that help was on the way. But God reminded me that I was looking for help from the wrong people, that those people weren't going to help me. Don't put your trust in man. You've got to trust God. I don't care how bad it is, don't look at the situation. Look at God. Put your eyes on Him. And I did that, thinking that these eight people would hear the facts of this case, the truth, and rule in my favor. Right! Wrong!

CHAPTER 6

After that was over with, I came home, I walked around, I followed my husband like a little girl around the house. I just was so close to a nervous breakdown. I knew I was. But there was just so much faith in me, knowing that I could not give up. I couldn't let depression set in on me because eight people said this man is not guilty. I don't care what eight people said, I know what this man did to me. And if I had to continue to fight, fight, fight, every chance, every angle, anything I could do to fight this thing, I was going to let them know that Pamela Smith will not go away like this. They thought when I walked out of that courtroom that it was over. Well, it wasn't over.

I contacted the State President of the National Association for the Advancement of Colored People (NAACP). He said, 'Ms. Smith, have you ever done a police report on this case?' I said, 'No sir.' He said, 'Well I want you to do one.' This was in February of 2004. I was raped in November of 1997 through May of 1998. I never had done a police report. The State President told me in February of 2004 to do a police report. That evening I got a friend named Patsy and we went to the police station on 36th Street North and filed a police report for the first time on this case. Now you tell me this wasn't a major cover up of a case. The next day I went to the police department and asked for a copy of that report, which was my birthday, February 6th. I don't even look at my birthday anymore. It has no meaning to me at all. All I can remember is being raped. Not a happy birthday since February 6, 1998. That's over with for me. If I could claim another day for my birthday, I would make me a new birthday and celebrate it, because February 6th has nothing significant to me at all anymore. It means nothing to me.

After I went to the police department and asked for a copy of the police report, I was told that you have to have a subpoena or a court order to get a copy. I didn't get to obtain a copy of my report. I don't know if that's a part of the system, or was that simply the way they were going to do Pamela Smith, continue to hide stuff on this case. I called the President and told him I made a police report. For some reason I called the District Attorney in Muskogee, Oklahoma and told him about my case and what was going on. He said, 'Well the statute of limitations is not out.' So that meant that I could still prosecute this man. Something the State should have done. Everybody should have prosecuted this man because I was in State's custody. I was awarded to the State and the State should have done this. But the State turned a deaf ear, hoping that I would go away, that nobody would believe me.

I thought about what he said so I contacted the State President of the NAACP again. He told me that a District Attorney, a friend of his, had told him, 'She needs to put a Grand Jury on that.' I thought about it, and I thought, boy, what do I do? How do I do this Grand Jury? So, I started putting a Grand Jury together. I made a couple phone calls trying to find someone that could do a Grand Jury because I had no knowledge of a Grand Jury. I didn't even really know what a Grand Jury consisted of. I heard about indictments and a Grand Jury but never dreamed that I would be bringing a Grand Jury to town or even trying to form a Grand Jury. I made a couple phone calls and got in contact with a lady attorney. I remember she used to work for the District Attorney's office and I asked her about a Grand Jury and she told me who the attorney was that does a Grand Jury. I took his name down and I thought about it, and I thought about it and I thought about it. In the meantime, I had contacted Senator Maxine Horner in February of 2004 and I said, 'Can you find out about this case for me, why it wasn't prosecuted?' I needed her to contact the District Attorney in Tulsa, Oklahoma. She made a phone call February 10th to the District Attorney's office and talked to him on the phone. He told the Senator that he never heard of me and never heard of this case. She said 'Well, I'm going to have Pamela give you a call.' The Senator told me to call the District Attorney, that he said he never heard of me or my case. That day, February 10, 2004, around four-thirty or five o'clock I called the District Attorney and I told him who I was. He was tapping on his computer, trying to find it. He said, 'I can't find anything about this case.' I said, 'Okay, well sir, I wrote you three letters trying to get you to help me prosecute this man back in '98.' He said, 'Well Ms. Smith, can you bring those letters to me so I can see them?' I said, 'Sure, I have no problem with that.' I told him I'd be there the next day. On February 11, 2004 I went to the District Attorney's office with the letters. I showed him the letters and he was shocked. I could see in his face that he was just devastated. He sat there and told me, 'Ms. Smith, we've got some pieces to the puzzle, but we need to get all the pieces.' I didn't really trust him because I knew that I had begged this man seven years ago to help and I heard nothing from him. My cry was ignored, ignored by the District Attorney. I cried from prison that I was raped and asked him to help me. He told me when he saw those letters that he never got them. That doesn't say much to me at all about District Attorneys to say that I never got those letters. That's not satisfactory information to me at all. I didn't accept what he said and wasn't really trying to hear what he was saying. I just figured that he was a part of the system and a part of this cover up on this case. That's just the way I felt. He said to me in this meeting that really just threw me backwards. I said, 'Sir, do you have the salt shaker?' He said, 'No ma'am, I sure don't. Then he said, 'Ms. Smith, could you contact the Lieutenant OHP Trooper and ask him for the glass salt shaker?' I said, 'No sir, I sure can't do that, because I'm not going to touch that glass salt shaker because they'll say I tampered with it or did something to it.' So I just simply did not want to be a part of touching that glass salt shaker and I couldn't understand why he would ask me to do that, unless he was trying to get me to touch it and tamper with it and then say, look she shoved it up herself or whatever because the glass salt shaker had not been seen since the Lieutenant brought it down to EWCC for me to identify in front of the DOC Investigator back in February or March of 1999. So I told him no. Then he asked me if I would call the First Assistant Attorney General, the lady that was representing the State Drivers Examiner to see if she would help. I told him no, I wasn't going to do that because they would say that I'm tampering with witnesses and trying to persuade people to lie and I wasn't going to do that. And then he said, 'Well, I thought maybe she would help you because she got off the case and she knew the case.' I said, 'That may be so but I'm not calling these people saying anything to them. You're the District Attorney and you need to do that.' I said, 'That's not a good idea.' He declined and said, 'Yeah, you're right.' So he declined to do either one, bother with the glass salt shaker or talk to the First Assistant Attorney General.

I left his office and ran into my probation lady and I was crying and upset because the District Attorney gave me no hope that he was going to help me. I really didn't go in there for help, I guess I was looking to see if he was really telling the truth or not, but he prayed for me. And when he prayed for me, I didn't receive this man's prayer at all. I looked up and could see horns coming out of that man's head. I saw the devil in that man and I didn't feel anything about that man's prayer. First of all, there's too many cases in Tulsa, Oklahoma that women are being raped and the cases simply are not getting processed. I just couldn't feel that man. His spirit wasn't there. My mother always told me to beware of people that prayed for you. Not everybody prays for you, because everybody isn't praying a prayer to Jehovah God for you. Some people could be praying evil upon you and serve the devil. So I didn't receive his prayer. I just wanted to see where he was coming from.

When I left there I went home and thought about it and I said, wow, maybe I do need a Grand Jury. I sat down and I thought about it and it came to me to do a video. I contacted the man that did my wedding and said, 'Can you come to my home and do a video?' He said, 'Yes ma'am, I can.' So on February 16, 2004 he came into my living room with his equipment and we filmed a video to send to the Governor of Oklahoma. I made this video and told him, 'Good afternoon, hello Governor. This is Pamela Smith. I was raped by one of your State employees' and I told him I was raped, there was no police rep, that I took a polygraph, our District Attorney told me that somebody came in his office and declined this case based on a piece of paper of a polygraph, which was the faulty polygraph that I talked about earlier, how somebody came in his office in March of 1999 and closed this case, and I asked the District Attorney himself, 'Why would you allow somebody to close this case based on a piece of paper opposed to a glass salt shaker with DNA, fingerprints and semen on this glass salt shaker?' He said 'I don't know, somebody in this office closed the case.' Now, I moved forward with this case. After I left the District Attorney's office I had a meeting with some friends at Metropolitan Baptist Church. We were going to form some type of help to help Pamela Smith, if it was to find the answers, if it was a strategy to move on with this case, to do what we needed to do to get some justice. I can recall Ms. Esther Vaughn and her husband there, Wilbert Collins, the NAACP from Muskogee's President, Reverend John Reed, Sr., Reverend Collier, my husband, my brother, some other friends, Ms. Carter, the lady that was trying to get attorney Bill Garton on the case. They were trying to bring civil rights leaders, everybody in. We had meetings trying to see what we could do to achieve in turning this thing around from this empty verdict that came January 13th from an all white jury in a civil rights case, 42 USC 1983 civil rights case. Liz was there. She came out and grandstanded too much. She came out and saw all these beautiful cars that the people were driving. We were talking about the appeal process on the case, and she was talking about doing an appeal and making her statement of how she made some mistakes and she knows that she learned a lot from this civil rights case. Maybe some fresh eyes need to look at this case and it wasn't something I was trying to hear simply because I was mad and bitter at her for calling me, trying to get me to take sixty thousand dollars and yet she stood up in front of my black friends and painted a different picture like she's all involved in this case. It was just totally different for me and I felt like had she focused more time on this case than the last three weeks of worrying about going on a ski trip and not preparing. She prepared it in 2001 and when she did, I think that's where she stopped because there were a lot of things she could have done differently in this case. But I realize that when you've got an all white jury and you just come with everything you've got, but a man is made up to do something like this, that's just the way it is.

After that meeting was over with I started trying to get money to get an appeal processed. In the meantime, my attorney filed a JNOV in a new trial to the Judge. They filed that motion in court. The State replied. Robert Martin replied again March 30th. On July 19 the Judge answered that ruling and denied me a new trial. He denied me a JNOV. Well, that was okay. In the meantime, I had prepared to bring a Grand Jury to town. I hired an attorney named Mike Smart in May and on June 7th I was granted permission to circulate a petition in Tulsa County to get signatures. I needed five thousand signatures. I took Mike Smart twenty-five hundred dollars cash to his office. His secretary received the money. He went to the Judge and told the Judge that I wanted the District Attorney recused from the case and the Attorney General's office. The Judge was trying to grant me that. The Judge allowed me to circulate a petition. June 7, 2004 he signed off. I went out to get the signatures. I worked the flea market every Saturday and Sunday to pick up signatures. I worked the convenience stores late at night. I knocked on doors until nine o'clock at night. I worked the fast food restaurant drive-thru, where people were ordering hamburgers and shakes and fries and salads. I was signing them up, telling them, 'Hi, my name is Pamela. I was raped by a State Drivers Examiner on 36th Street North. I was raped by instrumentation.' I said that so much that every time I said it, believe it or not, I healed just that much more inside. It brought me that much closer to my healing process. Not only that, I dropped some tears. I said it so many times that today I'm stronger. I am so much stronger. It was an experience for me to do the Grand Jury, to bring in this petition. However, I worked the last night. I needed five thousand signatures. My last night was July 22nd. I turned the petition in on the 23rd, went to Mike Smart's office with a friend and a friend of his. We walked up into the lawyer's office with a Federal Express box with all these petitions in it, seventy-four hundred, I believe it was. And all I needed was five thousand.

The lawyer said, 'Do you want to go with me? I can just take them down there.' I said, 'Yes, I'll follow you. I want to see this process myself, how it works.' So my friend and his friend and I got in my car and trailed this lawyer down to the courthouse and when we got to the courthouse, he walked up to the counter and gave them to this white clerk. Before I got there, the petitions were supposed to have been turned in on Monday, but two of my friends said, 'Don't turn that petition in early. All they're going to do is just mess with it and make a reason for this Grand Jury not to show up.' So I took their advice. But the black girls that work at the County Courthouse said that the white woman was saying, 'She ain't gonna get those signatures. She ain't gonna get them.' Well, I showed up with them two or three days after Monday, the day that they were expecting me to show up with them. You could have bought them for a penny, the white women. So after we turned in the signatures they went to the election board. And when they went to the election board, the election board certified to say they only had thirty-five hundred signatures. Now, I want to know, out of thirty-five hundred signatures, where are the other four thousand signatures? So, I fell short to bringing in a Grand Jury, but I got my hearings on August 4, 2004 for the jurors to have certified these signatures. I don't know which way this thing is going to go. I don't know which way it's going to play out. But it's not enough to stop me from continuing to fight. I still have an appeal process and this week I will be doing my appeal to the 10th Circuit Court of Appeal on this case, sending it back to Denver, letting the State know that they know this man is guilty of the things that he has done to me. So I will be going back to Denver with my new attorneys, Jones and Jones, who will be doing this case, Bob Black, the attorney, will be appealing me back to Denver, where I won in 2003. So I lost in lower court and there's something wrong with this picture.

I was contacted by the Social Security Administration on the 27th of July. I was sitting in my chair in my living room where I sit and meditate a lot. She said, 'Mrs. Hathorn.' (My name is Pamela Smith Hathorn. I got married but I still use Pamela Smith because of this case.) She said, 'This is Denise. My boss asked me to give you a call.' So Social Security called me to come in. I said, 'Well, I applied for this about three or four months ago, and I just didn't want to fool with it because I was busy with this case.' She said, 'Ma'am, my boss is an attorney that represents people for Social Security. This is your money, you need to come get it.' I sat there and I thought about it. I said, now you know, nobody but God because who calls you at seven o'clock in the evening, Social Security? It was a law firm that represents clients. So I said, 'Okay, I'll be there.' So the next day I went, told my story, cried to her and showed her all the articles that I had and she said that she was working on another rape case. She said, 'You have really been through a lot. Ms. Smith, there isn't anyway in the world you won't be granted your SSI on this case with all you've gone through.' Now I say this, that I was raped, I was forced, I was tortured, I was mistreated. I would do it all over again for a chance to see a family member and anybody that wouldn't do it for someone they loved don't love their family. You know, family is all a person has and when you don't have family, you don't have anything. So I just want to say, this case is far from being over, I am going back to Denver on this case. I will be filing my appeal this week. I did decline the SSI.

CHAPTER 7

Today the Senator Horner called me and said, 'Pamela, you only had thirty-five hundred certified signatures.' I said, 'Out of seventy-four, seventy-five hundred?' She said, 'Yes, that's what they said, registered voters.' Now, I'm not going to say that's true or not true. I know that since I've been a victim of nothing but a major cover up on this case, I don't trust anything from the State. I will keep going, and going, and going and going until God tells me it's over. I will persevere in this.

I want to back up and say, last Friday, August 30th, Candace Rowe and her mother met me at the *Okie Claw* to do her story for the first time in seven years. I got to the *Okie Claw* first, Candace and her mother had not arrived yet. When they hadn't arrived I got on my cell phone and called and said, 'Where you all at? I'm at the Claw.' They said, 'We're around the corner at the nutrition place. We'll be there.' They pulled up. When Candace got out of the car she was smiling.

Let me back up a little bit. In June 2004 I was knocking on doors getting signatures. It was late June. I knocked on four doors, and on the fifth door I knocked on Candace Rowe's auntie's door. I knew the young lady's name, Sherry. Sherry came out but I didn't know it was her. I was just getting signatures. I asked Sherry to sign my petition and told her what was going on. Sherry shared a story with me and told me that she was trying to get into the prison system, going in undercover, to see about some of these prison rapes, because she had received over twenty letters with ladies that had been raped while they were in prison but they didn't sign any names and she was trying to get in to help these girls. In the meantime she acknowledged to me that her niece had been violated by a man at 36th Street

North and she asked me his name. I shared his name and pointed out his picture. She said 'That's the same man that violated my niece.' I jumped for joy, shaken, crying. I couldn't believe that God had sent me straight to that young lady's house like that. For seven years I've always talked about Candace, but never knew who this young lady was. I always heard the State say 'She was forward, and she made that story up' and all that but I never heard her side of the story. So, I didn't bother to meet Candace, I just waited for God to set it up, although I was just one door from knocking on her door because I was at her auntie's house and Candace lived right next door. I didn't push it but I was very anxious, I was so anxious to meet this young lady, to just let her know that I'd been fighting for her for many years and that whatever it took, I was going to help her because she was a child and didn't know how to fight.

I went on home and was so excited about it. And there's one thing I found out about God through all of that. If I ever had doubt that God was real, He reconfirmed, reassured me that He was real, because that morning I asked Him to order my footsteps. I asked Him to take care of Candace and if there was any way possible that I could meet her. I had no clue that God was going to act as fast as He did in the same day. So it just let me know that even in fighting this case that God is so real. No matter how many doors are slammed in my face, God managed to open a window for me to just jump right out of, because the devil cannot hold down anything that belongs to God, and I do belong to God. So, I was so excited, I came home and I told my biggest brother R.L. what had happened, and I was looking forward to meeting Candace. Well in due time. Three weeks had passed when I finally got to meet Candace. It was a joy. She was everything that I just thought she was – beautiful, courageous, just so proud to meet me, as equally as I was to meet her. I met her mom and her grandmother. Just nice people. Just really down to earth people. A young lady that was just violated by a man that was trying to rob her of her innocence.

After that I prepared myself to start trying to get more signatures. I contacted a blues singer man that was a friend of Willie Jones and asked him if he would come in and help me sing. He said, 'Anything for you sis, I'll come in and do.' Vernor Garrett came in twice, in June and in July, and did two shows for me outdoors for free, trying to get people to come and sign this petition to help me bring in a second Grand Jury. I found out that so many people that were not on probation and parole were scared to sign that petition because they were afraid that the State would mess with them. I could not believe the ignorance that came from my race of people. I don't know if it's ignorance or just simply fear of a white man that is instilled on the people here in Tulsa, Oklahoma. I found out during this petition drive just how weak people were, how many favors people owed to the city that they couldn't stand up and help a wounded sister. I'm speaking of ministers, city officials. I can count the people that signed the petition that let it be known that they were standing by Pamela Smith's side against the State of Oklahoma. There was Bishop L. V. Broom, Senator Maxine Horner, Wilbert Collins, County Commissioner, Friendship Baptist Church, World One Church, Bishop Tyler, Bishop Harold Jones, Brother Warren Blakley, Pastor Sam Holmes there were people that were not afraid to come out and help me fight for justice. Here was a black lady raped in the heart of the black community, under the black people's noses. A little fifteen year old girl was violated. Another lady in the back room showing her body. Another lady who he made comments about her breasts. But yet the people in the heart of North Tulsa, the hood as they would say, still did not know anything about this case. And yet the lady that was raped, tortured, forced and mistreated was circulating the petition to help stop some of the abuse, stop the people downtown from abusing our people, raping our black women, sexual harassment on the jobs. This Grand Jury could come in and look at anything they wanted, but I had to educate my people as to what I was doing. Not simply to say that they were just not wanting to help, they were more afraid because when they would see a District Attorney or the Attorney General's office on this Petition, they would back up. And I had never seen anything like that. But God is good.

After I contacted my friend, Wilbert Collins, I said, 'Wilbert, I need some spiritual help. Do you know somebody, one of these ministers?' He said, 'Well there's a couple ministers that don't like me' and I said I understood that, and he said, 'I'd never done anything to Pamela, I'm going to give you Reverend W.R. Casey. Reverend Casey will help you, I believe he will.' Well, he gave me Reverend W.R. Casey's phone number and I called him. I was heading to Dallas with my brother on some business, so I called Reverend Casey on the phone. I said, 'Reverend Casey, this is Pamela Smith. I got your number from Commissioner Wilbert Collins.' He said, 'Oh yeah, yeah, yeah.' I said, 'Pastor Gates, I was raped by a State Driver's Examiner. My case is seven years old and I was raped, tortured and forced and threatened and abused by instrumentation of a glass salt shaker.' I told him the whole story and he started saying, 'Well, where is this man, where is this man?' like he was really going to help. In the middle of the conversation he asked me about Reverend Clark. 'Well what has Reverend Clark done?' I said, 'Well, he let me use his church to have a meeting in it.' 'Well what else has he done for you?' And I didn't know where he was going with that and I said, 'Well, he helped me organize people to come to his church for meetings.' So he said, 'Well, so Reverend Clark is standing by your side helping you?' and I said 'Yes and Senator Maxine Horner, and other ministers and some other supporters' and I said, 'The State NAACP President from McAlester, Oklahoma has been right by my side, giving me some help and direction in this situation.' And so he said, 'Well, I'm starting a newspaper. I don't have time to help you right now.' I said to him, 'Well you know what? If I was lining your pocket with five hundred dollars and inviting you over to a sister's house for chicken dinners, you would be willing to help.' He said, 'What did you say?' I said, 'I'll repeat myself.' I repeated myself and said, 'If I was putting five hundred dollars in your pocket and having you all over for chicken dinners, you'd be over to my house, trying to help a sister. But when you all found a sister that's wounded, crying out for help, you all can't help me.' And so I got off the phone with him and hung up. So I called Commissioner Wilbert and told him what the man said and he just said, 'Well don't fool with him anymore. I didn't know he was like that.' I guess a couple days or so passed, Wilbert and I talked on the phone again. We are real good friends and I said, 'Wilbert, how you doing?' So we talked, he said, 'I talked to Reverend Casey and he told me you were crazy.' I said, 'Crazy? Why am I crazy? Just because I told him that he didn't have time to help me, but if I was going give them five hundred dollars to line his pockets and invite him over for chicken dinner, they'll come over to a sister's house then?' Wilbert started laughing and said, 'Oh, that's why he called you crazy.' I said, 'Yes, I'm crazy for speaking the truth. If speaking the truth to these ministers, which these ministers in Tulsa, Oklahoma need to be spoken to, there's too many wounded people in Tulsa, with all these churches and all these ministers and all these cries for help, but they're not doing it.' So when I didn't get any help from Reverend Casey, later on I saw him at the courthouse. He was down there trying to sell his newspaper. So this guy called me over and said, 'Pamela, I've got somebody that can help you' and I said, 'Well, I'm busy right now. I don't have time.' I was reminding Pastor Gates that he didn't have time to help me and I didn't have time to be interested in his newspapers.

So after that was over with, Bishop Bell from Church of Faith, his wife, the first elect lady, stood up in her church and she did a dynamite speech there, encouraging people to sign this petition, stating how vital it was for our community. Not only was it going to help Pamela Smith but it was going to help our community. Sign this petition. I had left church early that day. I had been over to Antioch Baptist Church and spoke, and I left after getting signatures over there and ran over to Full Gospel Ministry and got signatures. After I finished getting signatures at Antioch Baptist and Church of Faith in the same day, I got on the radio with Harry and I talked and thanked the people for helping me and supporting me, my community for coming together. Well, after that was over with, I continued to go to a fast food restaurant at eight o'clock in the morning, stand in the line to get signatures on the petition, and I would be there until nine o'clock, nine thirty at night. My friends Sirretta, a young lady named Sheila, we all would hang up there. My friend, Cheryl Payne, came back and went out to Waterhouse Market. This white man told me that I would not be allowed to sign petitions at his location and I said, 'Okay, no problem. If I sit outside with a table and a chair, would that be permissible?' 'I don't want any of that.' Well just to show you how good God has been in this case, even with all the hidden injustice in this case, God still has His eyes on the sparrow, and His eyes are certainly on Pamela.

My friend called me that night, she came by a fast food restaurant, dropped her little girl off and they went out to the parking lot. I didn't know exactly where they were going. Well, next thing she called me and said, 'Girl, I'm at the Waterhouse Market and I got over a hundred signatures.' See, what man says no to, God says yes. The man told me on the phone earlier that we could not be out there but I didn't know where Cheryl Payne was going to go get those signatures. But she obtained over a hundred signatures out there in less than an hour. People were so eager to sign this petition, they were saying they were sick of the State of Oklahoma and how they're being treated. I have had so many women tell me their rape stories. I've had women tell me they were raped by their own fathers, I had a woman tell me that she was raped and shot and left for dead. I had a lady that came up to me at the flea market, lifted her blouse up and showed me where she was raped and thrown on the railroad tracks for dead, and showed me the track marks in her back. I have been considered by some people a hero for coming forward and standing up against my rapist. I figured that if you've got to live with this shame, and you've got to hurt and go through so much suffering in life because of somebody else's evil, I was not going to accept that. I'm a fighter, I don't quit, I don't give up. And I certainly know where my help comes from. I know who directs my footsteps and who tells me which way to go, and I knew, taking on the State of Oklahoma, representing this man, The State Drivers Examiner that raped me, tortured me, forced me, mistreated me. I have begged, begged the television stations to tell this story. Tell it. But they won't tell it because they know if they get on television, I'm going to cut them in two. I'm going to jump right in, so they'd rather not get on television, which keeps me from being able to tell my story, because the State of Oklahoma is definitely dictated by the Attorney General's office. Anytime you have this much news that's so informative to the community, especially the black community where I was known, where black people go to obtain their drivers license. The television people failed to tell this, simply just didn't want to tell it.

Last night as I was taping this interview for the Governor I found a little tape where I went into the Tulsa newspaper, sat down with a man named Michael, did the interviews with that man. I believe it was two hours with him, that interview has yet to be in the paper. None of this story has been told. And I can't understand how local Channel 2, 6, 8, any of these television stations, would have a daughter, a sister, a friend, a mother, a cousin, a grandmother, a son, anybody that was raped and tortured the way I was by a state worker, I know any of these television personnel or owners of these television stations would want this story told. They would have it on the headlines of their news. But yet, because I was black and I had a past, and based on the fact that nobody would believe me, but I have made it all the way. All the way for seven years, still telling my story. I believe in God that someday I, myself and Candace will be able to tell our stories. And I know there are many other women out there, simply because I know that that's why the State let this man go. They not only let him go because of Candace and Pamela, they figured that if there were two allegations made on this man, that there had to be other women. I was seriously abused, mistreated, raped, tortured and forced by instrumentation of a glass salt shaker. This man did everything he could to degrade me, hurt me, but it wasn't enough to make me stop fighting. I know that I should probably be somewhere in a mental institution, out of my mind, but I know because I serve a good God, a mighty God, a loving God, a gracious God, a delivering God, a healing God, a protecting God, that none of those things can touch me. No weapons formed against me shall prosper. I can do all things through Christ Jesus who strengthens me. I'm the head and not the tail; I'm above and not beneath; I'm the lender, not the borrower, and I can do all things through Christ Jesus. And this has just been a fight of my life, but I know when I entered this battle what God had promised me, and I'm still remembering God's promise.

CHAPTER 8

Today, August the 3rd, I went in there with my attorney, Justin Cooper with Jones and Jones. It was such a relief, even waking up this morning to the newspaper stating that I lost my battle to a Grand Jury short fifteen hundred signatures. That still didn't devastate me. It didn't knock me back or anything because my focus on this case has always been, always been my appeal process when I came out of that jury trial. You know, God is so good, back in January I was having meetings, I was trying to figure out how I was going to come up with ten thousand dollars to pay Jones and Jones to take on my appeal to take me back to Denver. My husband had a Peterbilt truck and that truck has given us nothing but problems trying to sell it. The title was all messed up, this person had a lien on it, but just when I spoke and said, God, I need ten thousand dollars, that title showed up today by Federal Express to where I was able to obtain the money to give the lawyers to take on my case. See, my thing has always been, if I go back to Denver, they can't help but read this transcript of this trial that took place from January the 6th through January the 13th . You would not believe what was wrong with these jurors, other than prejudice, other than they just didn't want to give a black woman her due process of the law and make this man liable for his actions. I thank God today that I was able to give the attorneys the deposit that they told me they needed to take me back to Denver. If I ever felt confident, I woke up two nights ago and prayed and said, God I need nothing but perfect peace. When Maxine Horner told me that I was short the signatures, my son Maurice called me today and said, 'Mom, you're in the newspaper.' Then my lawyer called me and said that I was in the newspaper, but what he had planned on doing, he said, 'Well Pamela, we can try and get another Grand Jury that's coming to town on another indictment to listen to your case.' I said, 'Mark, that would be great if you could do that.' I guess he thought that I was going to be devastated, depressed and sad that I didn't obtain the signatures, but you know, if I didn't do anything else, if Pamela Smith never did anything else in life, I know one thing, the State of Oklahoma knows that Pamela Smith's not afraid of them. They know I'm a fighter, I don't roll over and quit. They know that I know that this man raped me and I know the Attorney General knows this man raped me. I think that when somebody has a loved one that's incarcerated and a story like this hits home, you need to take note of everything that anyone is saying. Don't turn a deaf ear just because you're in a position and you don't want to rub your friends and colleagues the wrong way by making a righteous decision on the law. There is a righteous decision. And if they learn nothing else about Pamela Smith, that they first of all misunderstood me, misrepresented me, always counting me out and always, for some reason, thought because I was black and had a past, that nobody would believe me. For seven years, I may not have made the press in Tulsa, Oklahoma. The networks in the local cities are driven by political decisions on what to put on the news. If nothing else, they never learned that I don't quit. I don't quit to God, and right now God has not told Pamela Smith 'this case is over'. When I found out about the Grand Jury, I laughed. It was funny to me, because I know that the State Drivers Examiner hasn't had any sleep at night when he knew that I was trying to put an indictment on him. It was the anticipation to me of letting him know that he's never going to have any peace. He robbed me of my life, my joy, and some of my happiness, but that joy he thinks he robbed me of has been restored by God because my joy of the Lord, salvation, is on me and I would not let the State or anybody else ever intimidate me. Never. They can't intimidate me. And I hope today that this message, that I stood up and fought, wasn't just about fighting the State of Oklahoma, it was about hoping to send a message to women that when you're raped, you have to come out. Don't sit quietly. Fight back. When you fight you send a message to other men that, 'hey buddy, when you rape, these ladies are going to take you to court. They're going to expose you' and that's what my message has been about. And being that I came out so many people have said thank you. I can tell the women that were raped. They'll come up and hug me or they'll say thank you for what you're doing, or they'll just sign a petition. I see tears in their eyes because they're letting me know that somewhere in life they've been abused. And they're just proud that I could do that. They say, 'How do you do that?' I always say, 'Nobody but God. Nobody but God allows me to get up every morning and say hi.' I was raped by a State Drivers Examiner, tortured, forced, threatened and abused. I had a dying sister in the hospital. This man shoved a glass salt shaker in my vagina. I still have pain today because of this abuse this man inflicted upon me. I can still say that everyday and still find peace and joy in my life because God said, when you can't do anything else, He said just stand. And He said count it all joy. And through all I've gone through, I am so happy that I am still fighting the battle against the State, letting them know that I'm not a quitter. And I guarantee you this, as long as I have God on my side, the State would never, ever win. They may win a battle, but the war is not over. And God promised me. And I know God can do anything but fail, and right now I'm at so much peace when today, I met with my attorneys and gave them that money, I told them I am at so much peace. I don't care about the Grand Jury. I simply wanted a Grand Jury to come to prosecute this man, I did everything I possibly could to obtain those signatures. I was walking the street until ten o'clock at night, knocking on doors, hanging out at a fast food restaurant, running to the convenience stores, so beat that I had blisters on my feet, scorched my forehead from standing out in ninety-eight and one hundred degree temperatures at a fast food restaurant in the heat of the day, but I simply did all of that, but when I was told I ran short of signatures, that was not the goal I was looking for. My goal was my appeal to go back to Denver, and when God blessed me to have the money to go back, I feel so good right now. I know that the State of Oklahoma was nervous, shaking in their boots, when they knew I was a black lady, an ex-con, a crack head, but don't forget, whatever you do, don't count me out and don't forget, I am a child of God, that they were all nervous and shaking, hoping that I didn't get those signatures. But you know what? It doesn't matter. I sent a message loud and clear that I am not to be messed with. I am a fighter and I will, as long as God gives me the strength, the ability, the willpower, the fighting power, and the most important things, faith and trust, knowing that God is the head of my life, that I can do all things through Christ Jesus.

Today, I hung out with my grandson, Kyante. We bought a stereo and we've just been hanging out, having a good time. I met my brother R.L. for lunch today. We went to the Short Stop and just sat there and chatted and talked and after we left the Short Stop we went and got a pedicure. I told my older brother, 'Come on, let's go get a pedicure.' So we sat in the chairs next to each other and this made me feel so good. You know, even through all the losses of my sisters and brothers, I miss all of them, but my big brother is just a God-sent brother that I just thank God for. He deserves so much, so much, because he loves his little sister unconditionally, believes in me, and I just thank God that I have him. I will always see things his way, he'll always see things my way, but I'm his little sister and he always makes me understand the downside of things and he takes and dissects things and look at it. But I thank God for him being a man of God. And I thank God, I told him a couple days ago, I am so glad that where you and I are at in our lives with God today makes things so much easier for both of us. And I want to say to any woman that was raped, don't ever try to do this by yourself. Seek God first. Lean upon God. Depend on God. Pray and trust God for answers, hope, and direction through anything. If God brings you to something, He's going to bring you through it. If God called you to do it, He must have a plan to bring you out of it. So don't ever get to a point that when God calls you for something, you give up. When you give up, you will never know the end results. I'm just like the little old lady in Luke 18:1-7. In that verse it says: She prayed and didn't give up. Kept wearing the judge for justice, being persistent. She wore the judge so much that he said he had to answer because if he didn't answer, she was going to wear him down. Well that's what I'm saying to the State, 'I'm going to wear you all down. I've got a God that can energize me, give me strength to keep going when you all can't keep going. And all those people that you send in the courtroom, Mr. Attorney General, to come in there, sit on the stand and lie. Don't you want justice? Didn't you want to know, is it that important that you had to save the State money to let a black woman be misused and abused like this? I say this, what goes around in life, comes around. And when you lay down at night and you sleep, and you know that Pamela Smith was raped and tortured by one of your State employees, and you had an obligation to do something, you didn't. I guarantee you, God will fix this thing in due time. You may not see it, but it may come back on your children in life, but what goes around comes around in life. What goes up comes down. And I know Jesus will fix it.'

CHAPTER 9

When I came out of trial January the 13th, which was the trial that started January the 6th of 2004, I knew that I was going to do an appeal, and I knew that I was going to need my transcript to show how unjust this case has been, and how dirty the State has played to try to keep Pamela Smith from succeeding at any level on this rape case. Well I called this lady named Jo, the court reporter for the Judge at the Federal Courthouse, I told her I needed the transcripts so she told me that it was going to cost me three dollars a page, which was going to equal about three thousand dollars. I knew I didn't have three thirty dollars, let alone three thousand dollars at the time. So I said, Lord, that's when I got this group of people together, trying to come about this money for the transcript, because I knew that any lawyer that took this case would want a copy of that transcript. And I wanted to obtain a copy because that transcript was my key to victory back to Denver, and I knew this because I knew what happened in that courtroom, and all those mistakes and everything that the judge allowed these people to just say in the courtroom. I knew the answers were in this transcript and I put in my point that a transcript is just like a bible. It is your word and your testimony. And I knew all these people that sat on the stand and lied, I knew one day this transcript was going to come back and haunt the State of Oklahoma, especially if God allowed me to come up with the money to send this thing back to Denver. Well, this lady at the courthouse told me three thousand dollars. We talked for about a week or two. I built a little rapport with this little lady over the phone. I watched her in the courtroom during the minutes and taking notes during the trial, but when I needed this transcript, she let me know how much it was going to cost. Everything I ever had to do on this case, the price was high or the work was going to be so hard to do to succeed, anything to just discourage me. But nothing ever stopped me from just saying I'm going forward, because I figured if God brought me to it, He'll bring me through it. So, to make a long story short, I never did get the copy of the transcript, I never came up with the three thousand dollars at the time. Well I thank God, because from January to August 3, 2004, I got a chance to acquire just the ten thousand dollars. So, I called the lady at the courthouse on August 2nd and asked her, 'Did anybody order a copy of the transcript since the Judge denied me a ruling on the January 6th through the 13th jury trial?' She said, 'No, his clerk just worked from notes from the courtroom.' I got an overwhelming peace about everything that I was doing. I knew then, at that point when this lady had told me they worked from notes, it was on. I knew then God was getting ready to manifest things like never before because the devils were so sure of themselves with their notes that they didn't need any transcript. First of all, I know in a seven day trial there isn't a judge in the world, no clerk is going to remember everything people did in that courtroom, and believe me, there was a lot of wrong done in that courtroom. They allowed a lady to get up, off the stand, and go to the back and ask her family members to correct her on a date that she told under oath on the stand. This State Driver Examiner's wife made a mistake, gave the wrong date under oath, got off the stand, walked into the courtroom to her people, and the judge had left the courtroom. She went and asked her people and they told her the right date, she went back to the court clerk, up to the podium and gave them the right date. Now that's just one of many things that went on in this courtroom. They let my past come in, which early on Liz, the attorney had filed a motion in limine to keep my past from coming in, certain things the State of Oklahoma, the Assistant Attorney Generals just jumped up and did what they wanted to do. This was a trial that only you would have to see in a movie one day. That's how these people conducted this trial, a woman raped, tortured, forced and mistreated, and they didn't care. I'm going for the win, I'm going for the true justice and here these people in the courtroom are bouncing me around like I'm some kind of a ball. You know, going into this trial I knew I was going to be scandalized and talked about. I knew that. But I knew God was going to bring me through it. I never even worried about that. Whatever they said about me, all my life black people have been discounted. We have been scandalized, talked about and been misrepresented. So that didn't surprise me in the courtroom. I had already been prayed up, prepared my mind and soul that I was going into the enemy's camp. But I knew, sitting in the enemy's camp that God was sitting right there with me. I knew that in my heart. I knew that in my spirit. I smiled everyday, I looked good everyday. I held my head high, because I knew that God was sitting right there with me, directing everything that needed to be done. The way this trial turned out was the way God wanted it to turn out. He wanted it to turn out this way so He could get the glory. I probably did everything I said I was going to do, help my churches, my family, give to the community. But God wanted the glory through this. Had God given me that money, I wouldn't expose the devils like the devils need to be exposed, and right now, God is allowing me to expose these devils. I'm bringing them out, every one of them at a time. I've got them running into each other, I've got them confused, I've got them pointing fingers at each other, and I'm laughing. I'm rejoicing in the Lord because I know victory is mine in this case. But anyway, I would like to say that during this transcript, this lady at the courthouse told me on August 2nd, I believe, that the law clerk worked with notes from the trial. When I saw my lawyers on August the 3rd to give them the ten thousand dollar down payment to go to take my appeal back to Denver, I told my attorney and we laughed. I said, 'You won't believe this. This trial took seven days, you know there's a lot of mistakes in that trial, you know it came to me, especially when the judge couldn't hear and the microphone didn't work in the courtroom, they couldn't understand anything I or the man on the stand was saying. The microphone never did work clearly. I had to repeat myself over and over and over in this trial.' So when she told me they operated from notes, I knew then that they were just doing anything to keep Pamela Smith from succeeding. See, they got a copy of the transcript, I would be able to go down to the courthouse and obtain a copy of it because the original one has to be printed before you can get a copy. So what they did, they just didn't order any parts of it and worked from their notes. And the reason why they did that, they didn't think Pamela Smith was going to come up with three thousand dollars. They didn't even think Pamela Smith was going to be able to do her appeal, so they just took it upon themselves to say 'I'm sure of our notes. Our notes are accurate and we'll work from them.' How do you work from notes when there were nine hundred pages of a transcript? But I just thank God, and I was just showing how, in this case, it has been a battle after a battle. It just seemed like, really and truly, this has been one of the most racist cases, but I chose not to just play the race card or even suggest to go into the court and just offer all the racist things that were done to me during this trial. If my community and the world knows how this black woman was tortured, mistreated, and how this white man simply abused so many black women, and I can understand why the State simply let this man resign, because they didn't want the outcry of the community of other DPS agencies being alerted that there was a rapist working in their department, raping a woman in the storage room. So I just wanted to say that this case has been nothing but a bunch of injustice. It has been built on a lot of hidden injustice on this case. That's why today I stand to tell the Pamela Smith story. My rape, my case, my story.

Today is August 4, 2004. I started my day this morning with a prayer, talking to God.

I left my grandson and one of his friends here asleep this morning. As I headed to my business, approaching the courthouse around nine o'clock or nine-fifteen, I got a call from Don Caldwell, the guy who always stood beside me helping me with the petitions. He called to let me know that he was heading to the courthouse for my hearing on the petition drive. I got to the courthouse and sat in the hall, patiently waiting for nine-thirty to come. Around nine-twenty Don and Cecil and Sheila showed up. I sat there in a good mood, happy, just rejoicing and thanking God although I knew that we did not get all the signatures that we needed to bring in the Grand Jury. I sat there on the bench and told them that if we did do another Grand Jury, we had to be precise with registered voters and people living in Tulsa County. By that time my attorney, Mike Smart, walked up and told me that a Grand Jury was coming into town for this commissioner, trying to indict him, and there was a chance I could possibly get on that Grand Jury, but I might have to write a letter to see. We waited to go into the courtroom after Mike had talked to us. We entered the courtroom this morning and the judge said that there were not enough signatures, there was no way he could impound a Grand Jury. So we left the courtroom, went into the hall. We decided that if we did do another Grand Jury, what we would do differently to try to get a Grand Jury to bring prosecution upon the State Drivers Examiner, the man that raped me, tortured me and violated me repeatedly at 36th Street North DPS during November, 1997 through May of 1998. So after we talked to Mark I decided that we may go with another Grand Jury. We left and went downstairs. Cecil, Don and Sheila and I and the State President of the NAACP talked, just trying to get ourselves together, on what we were going to do different to achieve these five thousand signatures. We left in a good mood, happy and jolly. We were supposed to go to a fast food restaurant on Pine and Peoria, where Don and Cecil hang out everyday, just so thrilled about helping me prosecute this thing. I met them there and had a salad for lunch. I left there around eleven o'clock and went and met Senator Maxine Horner at Jabar Shumate's campaign headquarters. We sat there and talked and I asked her, 'Maxine, you're a Senator and have been a Senator for two decades. Why is it, I know that being black, it doesn't matter how much power we have, when a white man simply just wants to block us from succeeding, he would do anything he can. Why is it you can't get on the television, go to the people and ask to get this story told on television? This rape case. Why is it?' And she said, 'Pamela, it's just hard going up against an agency.' I said, 'Yes, but surely somebody would want to know this rape story. This story can help other women.' She said, 'I know. Now if I got drunk, being a Senator, they'll put that on the television. When we were in the Senate seat, Pamela, and someone acted like a fool on the floor, it'd be all over the television. But the positive things that we do don't seem to achieve, we don't get to get that type of achievement from the white man.' So I understood what she was saying.

I left there and went by Candace's grandmother's home. We sat there and talked about this case in general, what we expect to accomplish. We both are looking for prosecution for this man. Money's not important to either one of us, but if it's ours and it's due coming for the damages this man has done to us, it should be awarded to us. But prosecution is more important for Candace and myself. This man has violated us, did terrible things to both of us, and he should have been prosecuted, and we just are looking for true justice. That's all. And hoping that somebody will hear our cry and just quit ignoring it, and <u>begging</u> for somebody to tell this story, tell it on the television. Let the public hear what happened in the State agency. So we decided that we were going to try to meet with Mike Smart, the man that did the Grand Jury for me, to see if he could possibly get some criminal charges put on the State Drivers Examiner for what he did to Candace Rowe back on September 18, 1997, violated her first and then me in November of 1997. The guy never learned anything, just stalked Candace. She was young. I was an inmate and he thought he could get by with it. And darn near think he's gotten by with it, but he hasn't. God is still in charge.

I left Candace and I met with my brother and we talked. We had lunch at a Mexican restaurant, he and my grandson and I and one of Kyante's little friends. I asked my brother to go with me at five-thirty to meet with the lawyer with the law firm Walters, Walters & Jones, with Candace and her mother and grandmother, and he agreed to do it. After I picked up my brother at four-thirty, we went and picked up Candace and her grandmother and Candace's baby. We headed to the law firm, met Candace's mother, there. Well, we went in, sat down and talked to Mike Smart and that is one of the most negative attorneys I ever met. He tried to tell me eight thousand signatures is a lot to get, it's an uphill battle, anything to try to discourage me from doing the Grand Jury. He asked me and everybody else to excuse ourselves out of the room, that he wanted to talk to Candace by herself, which I can understand attorney-client privileged information. He said nothing positive to this young lady and she has high spirits, high hopes. We both are realistic women and we know and understand the law very well. And I think that she was hoping to get some prosecution on this man. Mike Smart reminds me of a person that truly, underneath it all, doesn't want to see us black women succeed in this case. However, I'm saying that, and the reason why I say that is because of how he tried to discourage me and this young lady from going forward. I know there's power in numbers, and if I talk about what happened to me and this young lady talks about what he did to her, there's collaboration right there to support both of our allegations. And I don't know, I just never felt comfortable with him, trusting him enough to allow for everything for me on this case. The Grand Jury, he told me how hard it was, how expensive it was and everything was negative. Nothing positive came out of that man's mouth. So after we left his office we stood outside and talked, and I told him before I went outside, that I don't care what he says, I trust God for everything, and everything that he has told me negative, God has done something different. He said, 'Well, eight thousand signatures is a lot to get.' I said, 'We've got seven thousand. They may not have been the correct signatures, registered voters in Tulsa County, but we achieved numbers. So there's nothing hard about getting eight thousand signatures when you've got a determined mind and you are willing to fight and seek justice.' So I felt a little bit uncomfortable with that lawyer. Like I said, as we moved outside, all of us, my brother R.L., Candace, her mom and a friend, and the grandbaby, we stood there and talked for a moment and Candace's mom said, 'It's all about where you trust God in what you're doing' and I agree with that.

So after we finished talking, we got in our cars and went our separate ways. My brother and I went back to our business and let the workers out, locked up for the evening, went to the store and bought some videos and bought my brother a stereo cassette player. After that I went to a café and had a meal with my brother and we sat and talked some more. I spend a lot of time with my big brother. My big brother is a balance for me. He shows me when I'm right and wrong and he doesn't have any problem saying it to his little sister, and I like that, because when he gives me advice it's constructive criticism, which I take to heart because when people love you they'll tell you when you're wrong and not allow you to continue to make mistakes and show you your fault. And he pointed mine out and I like that about my brother. And he'd do it with love when he did it.

After that, I took him home for the evening and just for relaxation I went out to Catoosa and played some slot machines. Earlier today I blessed a lady with fifty dollars that I know she needed, with two kids. And I'm a firm believer, when you bless somebody else, God blesses you. I went out, really for relaxation, if it could be interpreted to say, it's therapy for me to just take my mind off of all I've had on my mind on this rape case. But I thank God that when I won the sixteen hundred dollars, I told my brother and shared it with my brother. So, just a blessing, and I'm grateful to God for what He's always given me. I don't count the money I have in life, I count my blessings. I have more blessings than I do money and it's more important for me to have more blessings than money. Blessings keep you in touch with yourself and blessings always keep you mindful of what you didn't have and what God is doing for you in your life. And I thank God for that. Money, it's okay to have, being that I've had money and wasn't happy with it. I haven't had millions and millions of dollars, but I've had my share of money. The Bible says 'A fool and his money will soon depart' and that's what happened to me. I'm happy, just who I am in Christ today. I told my brother earlier today, I am so thankful to God for where he and I are at in our lives with God, because I am so thankful, knowing that when things don't go right in my life, I can call up on God and He will never turn His back on me or my brother.

I came home and just relaxed this evening and ended my day about twelve-thirty. I talked to my husband Eddie several times today. My sweet husband, a truck driver, that I adore so much and I thank God for Eddie, a good husband, a wonderful man. A sweetheart.

CHAPTER 10

Today is Thursday, April 5, 2004. I saw Carolyn today. She typed a letter for me to send off to Jerry, asking him to help Candace Rowe and me on this case against the State Drivers Examiner who has violated us and there has been no help, no exposure on this case. Carolyn prepared the letter, I talked to the lawyer that's doing the Grand Jury for me, and possibly for Candace Rowe. He told me that the statute of limitations was not out on Candace Rowe's criminal part and that we had a chance of her being a part of this Grand Jury. He also told me to bring him some more money to impanel a Grand Jury again. This was my second time attempting to do it. I know that the second time around is sometimes better and I'm looking forward to getting out and obtaining the five thousand signatures that we need of Tulsa County residents and registered voters. I met with my adopted father, Bishop Broom, a man whom I respect and look up to as a man of God. When I was wounded I went to him, crying my heart out for help and he has just been standing by my side, doing whatever he can as a man of God, and accepted me as his adopted daughter, a wounded daughter I would say, and we sat down and visited today about putting a minister program together so we can bring in all the ministers in a sit-down dinner to let these ministers hear what I have to say in trying to obtain these signatures. I need the help of my black ministers, their church congregation to help us get these signatures and get this thing done the right way this time. Of all the things I've learned doing that first petition, of jealousy, lack of knowledge of my people, fear, ignorance, a lot of anger, I learned a lot, witnessed a lot, heard a lot. So many different stories about everybody that had a son in jail, a daughter in prison, or somebody's been harassed by the police, and this is an opportunity for everybody to benefit from this. There's two hundred thousand black folks in Tulsa, and there was no reason for me to have to do this again, but whatever God tells me to do, I will do it. It's amazing how God has just used me to keep going. I know I'm on a mission for God. I know I am. Here I didn't obtain enough signatures to do a Grand Jury and now here I am, having an opportunity only from God, that would allow Pamela Smith to do something like this. So I'm just thankful for that. I visited Bishop Broom today, talked about some of his plans and his dreams and I know God is going to manifest for this man because I know he's a true, true man of God who loves God, loves people. He's probably been misunderstood and misrepresented by people, but anyone that's doing something positive and somebody that loves God, people will always have a desire to misunderstand the man or miscalculate the man, dismiss them and denounce them for whatever reason or defy them on their own terms. But this is my father and I thank God for him. He sat down today, he talked to Jabar Shumate and let Jabar Shumate know that he would commit to supporting him. And I thought that was very outstanding because he showed a lot of integrity to me when he told Jabar and me sitting at that meeting today, that I'm a man and I commit. I stand by that commitment. Not because of what friends here do, he didn't break his word, and I liked that because that shows that a man that makes a commitment, has some directions in life, and he has some strength. He built things by following through with them and I could see all of that wisdom in my pop, I can see all the love and a lot of God in this man. Nobody but God, as I always say, nobody but God. Those are my favorite words, nobody but God. No matter what it's been, nobody but God.

After we had that meeting, I told Pastor Broom, 'Give me your robe, I want to take it to the cleaners and get it cleaned' and he let me take his robe. We sat down and decided that he was going to call Pastor Tisdale at Friendship Baptist Church to see if we can have the sit down dinner there and all the ministers, on a Monday night, so that's what we were looking forward to doing there. I left there and made another phone call to my attorney, Mike Smart, and he again indicated that Candace's statute of limitations was not out and I told him, 'Just go ahead and do whatever you need to do because I need to start getting this petition drawn up.' So that's where we're at with this petition.

I'm leaving for Mississippi in the morning. I had Kyante here today and his mom picked him up this evening. My brother R.L. came over this evening, talked to my husband several times today, my wonderful husband Eddie. I went to Social Security today and to my disappointment I found out that my husband made too much money and that I could not draw disability or SSI, but I certainly hope and pray that whatever my denial was for Social Security, it was okay because I don't need to depend on anything from anyone but God. So I thank God for that. And the people God wants me to depend on, He'll put in my path. He would definitely do that. So, a little disappointment. I talked to Candace and her mom tonight, and Candace is upbeat about finally getting some justice for herself on what happened to her. So anyway, I had a blessed day today, but all is well. God says 'When you can't do anything else, stand.' And everyday I counted all the joy. Everyday I counted all the joy. I don't care what it is, I counted all the joy because I know where my help comes from. I know who I lean and depend upon. Nobody but God.

I went by a fast food restaurant today where we did the petition drive, saw Don Caldwell, the gentleman that just became a brother to me through all of this fighting that I'm doing on this case with the State. We sat there and figured out, making sure that when we do this second petition, what our plans are and where everybody's going to be, then we visited for awhile. After I left I got in my car and a lady named June Click from Fox 23 called me and left messages on my cell phone. I returned her call today, August the 5th, and she asked me about still doing the show on the television, airing our case, and I told her, 'You all have enough information to air this on the television, why are you all still calling me, asking for documents? If you want some documents or need something, you have enough.' She said she was waiting on my lawyer, Mike Smart, to give her the investigative report on this case from DPS, that they were supposed to get it on the State Drivers Examiner, Candace Rowe and Pamela Smith, and she wanted to see that report. However, today Mike told me he had not gotten it yet. So, Fox 23 calling today kind of surprised me because we've been begging all these local news stations to tell this story, and yet it has not happened, in Tulsa, Oklahoma. Rape has no color. It has no respectable person, so I just hope and pray that one day the Attorney General can search his heart and see that this was not anything near true justice on this case at all. But I'm going to keep on pushing, keep on believing in God, keep turning every rock and stone over that I can, and I will not let up. I will not give up. I will not give up until God says it's over and I know God is not saying it's over. I'm prepared for the long haul, I'm prepared for the battle, mentally, physically I'm ready.

CHAPTER 11

Today is Friday, August the 6th. I took some voter registration forms to Don at a fast food restaurant to get ready for our petition drive that we're going to do again to bring in a Grand Jury, my second time around. We're going to register people to vote, and I saw Don at a fast food restaurant and we're both upbeat about doing this petition because even in the midst of my storm I still find joy, and I laugh, but I hurt inside but I don't let anything steal my joy. I left Don and I went by Candace's today and picked up her story which she gave to me so I would be able to release it to the press or whatever I wanted to do with it. I visited with her for awhile, we talked about her being on the Grand Jury Petition, that her name should be included, and I agreed that her name should have been included. The lawyer told me that he needed some money from her and I told him, 'Don't worry about that. Just go ahead and put that child's name on that petition. She doesn't have any money, I'll take care of it.' He said, 'Okay.' I talked to Candace and told her that I'd taken care of her finances as far as her being on this Grand Jury Petition. Her voice needs to be heard. This man was going to rape her. The fact that he shut that door and locked it and suggested comments to her for anything other than not showing this young lady decent respect, I thought that her name should be on this petition as well. It should have been on the first petition, but I didn't know Candace as well as I know her now, and didn't know what her circumstances were. I've been fighting for her for seven years, calling her name out to God, talking about her in all my news stories that I do, they videos I do, I've always talked about Candace. She's a little sister to me.

After I left Candace's today I went by the flea market and saw Judy and her husband. I asked Judy if I could have another booth there to register people to vote and she said I could. I paid her to rent the booth for five weeks and she was glad to have me back. I told her that we had to do the petition over because I had seventy-four hundred signatures, but only thirty-five hundred of them were good. We needed them all to be registered voters and live in Tulsa County. I'm grateful that I still have people that are still standing with me and want to see justice on this case.

After I left there I went to see Bishop Broom. I picked up his robe today, the pretty white robe I had cleaned. He's just like a father to me. I picked it up and I bought it to mom, Mom Broom, a watch and took it over to Papa Broom and gave him his robe. We sat there and visited and talked about August 23rd when I'm going to put on a dinner for the ministers and friends to come out and hear my story of my rape and torture by this man, the State Drivers Examiner on 36th Street North, and also to hear Candace tell her story for the first time. So I sat there and visited with Pop. We talked a little bit about what to expect and he was going up to Pastor Ragsdale's church, Friendship, to confirm that we could do the 23rd of August, for all the ministers to get together to take the petitions back to their churches, to their congregations and get everybody to sign it. After I left there I went to the store. I had Candace's story copy that she had written to Opal and Jerry, telling her story for the first time. I made a thousands copies of Candace's story and it's a very heart wrenching story, a very sad little story, and today she still suffers and hurts behind that. After I left there I got in my car and called a white lady named Belinda who worked for the *Okie Claw* and by all indications everybody says the *Claw* is not owned by blacks anymore. I don't know that that's true or not but I talked to Belinda about doing an ad in the paper for thanking the community for supporting me and helping with this Grand Jury Petition, however we needed to do it again. I asked to speak to Sammy and she said he was not in. She told me that an ad would cost thirty-five to fifty dollars to put in there with a hundred words. I also asked her why Candace's story wasn't printed in the paper when she did it last Friday and she said would ask Sammy who said he couldn't run it right now, for whatever reasons I don't know. It seems to me like it's somebody dictating to that paper's will what to do and what to put in and what not to say. Here's a black newspaper in a black community, been in the black community, owned by blacks and now all of a sudden we can get raped in our community and our own black people can't tell the story the way the story is. They pick and choose. I did a story with the *Okie Claw* and the interview that I gave was nothing like what they printed in the paper. The young lady did a fine job but it wasn't telling how I was raped with this glass salt shaker. It wasn't telling how I was tortured. It wasn't telling all the things this man did to me like taking another lady and me to a park. I did that in my interview but it was not in this *Claw* story when this young lady did my interview. She wrote it just like it was writing a story for a, I don't know, it was a nice story, it got a lot of response, but it didn't tell the whole story. It didn't even touch my story of all the pain and suffering and force and threatening that this man, the State Drivers Examiner, has done to me and how he did this other little girl. So we both did stories for the papers but for some reason I often wonder, have these stories landed up in maybe somebody else's hands other than the purpose of telling the story for the community to know what goes on in their own community? So I don't know where this story's at. It's just like that tape that I did for Channel 81. Barbara says she couldn't find the tape. She doesn't know where it's at. I asked her for a copy and she said she couldn't find it. It's strange how we give interviews and they never show up on the television or really in the newspaper the way we tell it or what we say, you know. It shows up, it did in the *Claw* for me, but it wasn't everything that I said. They said my story was too graphic for them to print. Well, I told the truth. I told it like it is. It needed to be printed no matter how graphic it was. The fact that they need to let mothers know and fathers know that they've got daughters going in these DPS places where men are working and doing their driving tests with these ladies and mothers. So I felt like they needed to know the truth. It was graphic but it needed to be told. And me telling the story, as painful as it was, I did it hoping my story would help others. But no, they seem to think they're going to close this chapter. They're not closing this chapter on Pamela Smith.

After I finished talking with the lady on the phone at the *Okie Claw*, I went over and talked to Sassy, who is married to the son of the Greens who own the *Okie Claw*, a dear friend of mine. She and I went in a room and we talked and I asked her what was up with the *Okie Claw*. When we take information over there it's not being printed and she indicated to me that a black paper that was once owned by blacks, we don't know who owns it now simply because there's more white people running that paper in that facility than the Greens themselves. But anyway, after I left there I got angry so I took Candace's story to the Full Gospel Church. I'm going to put her story out there. I also faxed her story to Opal. I followed it up by trying to call Megan today, but she was out until the next week. I also overnight expressed my story and her story to Jerry, asking him to please air our story and help us. Begging different people hoping that things were going to turn around for Candace and me on this case. We both were looking forward for the Grand Jury coming. All we both are looking for is true justice. If it means to lock this man up and throw away the key, then that's true justice. Right now I haven't seen true justice. I would like to see the District Attorney, the Lieutenant, the Attorney General, DOC, Lanee Black, all these people that failed to help me and failed to help Candace Rowe. I want them all, in some way to know what it's like. I don't want anything like this to happen to their wife or daughter or sister or mother, but I want their conscience to bother them so bad that when they lay down at night to sleep, my name just eats at their conscience, Pamela Smith, Pamela Smith. Why didn't you help her? Why didn't you help her? Why didn't you do the right thing? I want the same thing for Candace Rowe, that their conscience eats them up with guilt that they should have helped her. Not because we were black females and especially a young girl, fifteen and an older woman that was locked up and he thought that nobody would believe us. And what's so sad is that the State went right along with all of that. You know, trying to cover this case up. That's why I call this hidden injustice. It's nothing but a bunch of hidden justice on this case. A lot of lies, cover-up and it's been a major fight for me. Every time I get over one hurdle, there's so many of them trying to cover up evidence and lie. But I know God is a force of one. I know that and I know who directs my footsteps daily.

On August 8, 2004, my brother R.L. was not feeling well so I saw about him yesterday. Also I visited with Candace, her mom and grandmother yesterday, just talking in general about the case. All the things that I've gone through. Today I got several hundred copies of Candace's story because the press refused to tell our story or help either one of us with these allegations against the State Drivers Examiner, so I decided to take it upon myself. I know how to lean and depend on God and myself. So Candace wrote her story out to Oprah and I'm hitting the streets, putting this story in everybody's hands that I can. I thank God that we have an opportunity to spread the word and the community is so hyped up about this second Grand Jury. Everybody's ready to sign the petition though they didn't sign the first one. Everybody's excited about it, I thank God for that.

Today is Sunday, August the 9th. I got up and prepared to go to church this morning. I was kind of troubled in not knowing which one I wanted to go to today. To my church, Greater Love Temple or Full Gospel Outreach Ministry. I love my pastor, he's such a gifted speaker and it seems like everything that he preaches has my signature all over it, of things that he's gone through that I can witness myself. When your family and friends turn their backs on you or when you think you're standing alone, you're not. You've got Jesus standing with you. Just all the things that I've gone through. I admire my pastor because he's gone through so much of the same things that I've gone through. The only thing different I don't believe he's ever been raped. He's been in prison and he promised God that he would serve Him. He's certainly doing that. A wonderful message today. I went down for prayer today and my Pastor told me that my brother Kermit and I love each other. We do. We've just got some problems. My little baby brother's on drugs and he knows the word but he just strayed away. He's probably what you'd call the Prodigal Son and I was the Prodigal Daughter but I made my way back in and I'm just praying and asking God to let Kermit make it back in. Come on in. You know, we all have bases in life but we all sometimes stray away from them. But when your parents instill those good things in you, I don't care how far you stray away from home, you come back to bases, what your parents taught you and instilled in you. And our parents instilled a lot of good things in us. And I think that my baby brother's and my problem is, we both are so spoiled and hot headed and we both are fighters. Just true fighters. You know, all my brothers and sisters were fighters. We all have our own way of fighting things and I think this has been the ultimate test for the Brannon clan. This one here is for little sister to take on but I know that I can do it because I know God is in control, not me. I'm not running anything. God is just dictating everything, ordering the footsteps, just making sure that all things are just the way He ordained it to be. And I'm thankful for that.

After church today I went and got my brother some soup. He didn't feel good today, so I took him some soup and he was still in bed. I saw Barbara Winslow on the television at my brother's house. She had on this dress that seemed like it had three or four tiers on it and she had her husband come on stage and she said everybody's got to have somebody to have their back, and she was talking about her husband has her back. When she was preaching the word and saying that being violated because you weren't covered or you weren't probably under the will of God, I gave all my attention to that television program at that particular moment because it made me realize that what happened to me. Had I been under the covenant of God, that never would have happened to me. So I thank God because I know now that I'm ordained by God to go through this because there's a purpose of me helping someone else. It's not designed for anyone but Pamela to have gone through this because God knows my strength. He knows my weakness and because He created me, He knows that I can stand this. My pastor told me today I was tired but I wasn't tired of fighting. And he's absolutely right, I'm not tired of fighting this case. I can't begin to get tired. I'm nowhere near tired. The State may have more money than I've got but I doubt they've got the patience and the King Justice, Himself on their side. My Father is head of any judge, any justice system, Supreme Court, my Father is the Supreme Court. He is the head of heads. And so I don't get tired. I won't get tired. So, like I said, they may have more money and can beat me that way, but I'll be darned they'll beat me with my patience, because I've got the patience of Jobe. I can wait it out. Wait it out, and I will.

After I left my brother's I went by the office, wrote some letters, got some information prepared for a paper.

CHAPTER 12

Today is Saturday, August 28th. I worked the flea market today, got quite a few signatures. The Channel 81 TV station came out and interviewed me. The gentleman asked me questions that just kind of threw me backwards about DNA, which confused me because they're supposed to be talking about petitions but since he wanted to go to that level, I went there with him. That was around three or three-thirty today. Sunday I went back out to the flea market and got more signatures. I missed church because I'm just kind of pressed for these signatures, working hard trying to get it together. Sunday night around nine o'clock p.m. my husband Eddie went into the hospital with chest pains and shortness of breath. That night I slept on the sofa at the hospital in the hallway to be with my husband because he was not in a private room. The next day I got up and requested a private room for Eddie and later that day they moved him to one, which was that Monday. I ran out doing signatures, just stressed, tired from the hospital. It's been a real hard week for me, checking on signatures at a fast food restaurant with Don and then went back and found us a new location. A white man at a grocery store was complaining about being offended because we were saying that a State worker raped me and this man worked for the State. But we had been at that grocery store for two months and this black guy, the store manager, had no problem with us sitting out there getting signatures, not bothering anyone, just trying to obtain signatures to impanel the Grand Jury, being fair about it, saying we were just trying to get the case investigated. But this white man went in and complained to a white manager and the white manager made Don move. So when they closed that door, God opened another one. We moved right over to the Shop-A-Lot that Monday evening. I didn't even sweat it. I just said, 'Don't sweat the small stuff. Don't let white people get under your skin like that because that's just a way to try to keep us off the focus point of getting these signatures.' I know that when the devil starts messing, that God has got a blessing. I understand that. So we moved over to the Shop-A-Lot that Monday night. After I finished getting signatures I went back to the hospital so beat, so tired.

Tuesday morning I got up and they told me my husband had to have surgery, which he did. They went in and put a stint in his heart because he had three arteries closed, and they went in and opened up one of his arteries. It was eighty percent closed. I thank God that my husband made it through that. I stayed at the hospital, went out and got signatures, back and forth to the hospital, just stressed, so worn out. This went on Wednesday, Thursday and Friday, back and forth from the hospital to the signatures. They signed the signatures until eighty-thirty and nine o'clock at night then I rushed back to the hospital.

Friday I brought my husband home from the hospital. I believe it was Thursday or Friday, I'm not certain. I'm so confused on days, but I believe it was Friday that I checked him out of the hospital and brought him home. He hadn't been feeling well but God is good. I know God is going to bring him through this. I met a man named Steve White who came over to the flea market on Saturday morning to meet me. He owned Cheap For Less. A God-sent man. Not only a nice man but a man that came with money to help me with finances, to help me take some of this burden that was kind of heavy on me from missing payments on my house and just robbing Paul to pay Peter. This man didn't know anything about me but he put a fifty dollar bill in an envelope and gave it to me. It was just a blessing. I was thankful to God. I didn't ask for it but I thank God for that. He offered to let me sit at his Cheap For Less right next door to the Good Citizen Flea Market and get signatures. We hauled up and went down to his store and I got signatures there. And I thank God for Steve White, he's just been outstanding.

Today is Sunday, September 5th. Steve White came to the flea market while I was getting signatures today, wanting to help. What do I need? And he's working on the prison ministry. He's a man that loves God and I love God and I thank God for what God has done for me and where I'm going in my life. With this case, as far as I can go with it, as far as prison ministry, I will go as far as God will take me with it and until He tells me that He has something else He wants Pamela to do. And I will be obedient to God because whatever God has called me to do on this case, to help people, to educate people, to bring people out of bondage of being raped in prison and stop the abuse that goes on. Inmates die, their medical needs are being neglected. I certainly would like for God to continue to bless Steve for his ministry and I want to be a part of his team because he's a man that sincerely is not looking for anything but people to be treated right and fair in the prison system. So we talked today. We visited today about some things in the upcoming week, commercials and concerts and dinners for the churches and inmates' families coming together and just doing things. So I thank God for that and praise God for Steve coming into my life. I got about three hundred fifty signatures between Saturday and Sunday this week. Between Saturday and Sunday I registered about eighty-two people to vote. And I thank God for that.

Monday, Labor Day. At six o'clock I cut a commercial at Cheap For Less. It took me at least seven or eight times to get it right. I cried during the commercial, just reliving this rape all over. Steve White gave me a place in his store everyday that I needed to get these signatures. The people at Cheap For Less have been very receptive to helping me and I have sat there and collected signatures daily.

My husband will be going to the doctor today. I'm going to the radio station. Today is Thursday, September 9th. I'm going to do a commercial at the radio station KCAA with Steve White. I thank God for this man, he just came on board and has been a blessing to me. I'm just grateful. Today is Thursday as I indicated. I will be back at Cheap For Less after I do my commercials at the radio station today.

Today is Saturday, nine/eleven. What a blessed day. Everybody that came in Cheap For Less or I met at the flea market down the sidewalk from the store were just Christian people. Everybody seemed to lay hands on me, wanted to pray. And I know, I know yesterday that God was so in the midst of this petition drive that it's so unreal. Women were just coming from everywhere to sign the petition on Saturday, nine/eleven. Just a blessed day. God's anointing, His presence was so real with the people and me, three sisters, black ladies came in the flea market. One that praised me earlier and went back. She had heard me on the radio the day before. And she told her sister, 'Sharon, I think this is the lady you used to model for, Pamela Smith. She's on the radio, you've got to hear her story.' So this sister went and got her sister and another lady and they came to the Cheap For Less, standing around my table. And what I saw in those three sisters were the three sisters that I lost, Elweeder, Esther and Diane. And God will certainly bless you and send what you need. God told you He'll help you. He didn't say when, how and who it would be. He said He'll help. He will send help. And I thank God for His word. These three ladies prayed for me, they anointed and their mother was there with them. It was just a blessed time. A lady that ran for Senate and her friend stopped by the table, it was just uplifting. She was telling me to forgive and, you know, just uplifting, words of encouragement to keep going. And I just thank God that I know that the Grand Jury belongs to God. And I thank God for the opportunity I had. My husband helped me work. Candace's came out and sat around the tables and I just thank God, for yesterday was a very anointing and blessed day. I thank God for Steve White for putting me on the Christian station and allowing me to be able to speak to the public about my case.

On September the 14th my attorney called me and I had a lady named Judy in the car. She was helping get signatures for this other Grand Jury that was going on. He called me and said to me, 'Pamela, the State offered you twenty-five hundred dollars to settle the case. I told him to kiss my rear and bend his momma over and kiss her rear too. And I told my attorneys 'Don't ever call me with crumbs and don't insult me' and that I had paid ten thousand dollars to do this appeal on this case. Why would I settle for two thousand five hundred? So I told him anything from now on at that point I want everything in black and white writing, sent to me. Also I went down to the courthouse yesterday and got signatures from the county courthouse, got a lot of response. I went to a grocery store and got some signatures. I also worked at Shop-A-Lot on Pine and Lewis and got a lot of signatures. I'm approaching my deadline but I know God is able and I know that I used some foul words but I am a Christian lady and sometimes you step out of the flesh because the devil can really take you there but you have to remember, don't let him carry you there. And so if he carries you there, just don't stay there. You know, have enough sense and enough God in you to come back. But I thank God that things continue to move on. When the State offered me that money, that was just a sign of a confession to me. I don't care if it was a penny, that's admitting guilt that they know this man raped me and I've been saying all along I know the State of Oklahoma knows Pamela Smith knows that they know this man is guilty. I know that. So I had a good day. I saw my brother yesterday and talked to my son Maurice, so everything is just going great, as God planned. And I talked to Steve White several times, told him what the Attorney General's office supposedly had called to offer me, twenty-five hundred dollars to settle a ten million dollar lawsuit. I guess they really think black people are so desperate and don't understand the value of money.

Giving honor to God whose head of my life. September the 17th I was contacted by my attorneys that Channel 1 wanted to do a story on me. And I in turn called Channel 1 and talked to a lady named Ageeda Neil, and she kind of like pleaded for me to give my story to them. And I told her that I <u>begged</u> them for seven years, seven months to tell this Pamela Smith rape story and they ignored my cry. It made me suspicious, 'Why do you want my story three days before my Grand Jury Petition is to be due, turned in?' So I didn't feel comfortable with them, I declined. She called my lawyer back and my lawyer wasn't in but she talked to the secretary so I called the secretary and she said, 'This lady called me back trying to influence us to get you to do a story.' I said, 'First of all, did you tell them that my lawyers don't tell me what to do?' And so therefore she said, 'Well, no, we just let them know that's your choice.' Well anyway, I called the lady back and I told her, I said, 'Let me tell you something. You're not out here helping me getting signatures. All you're interested in is doing a story.' And I said, 'And at this point I don't trust Channel 1 simply because I know you aren't just trying to get my story on the television, you'll try to wreck it anyway you can because the media can be bad for you.' It could be your best friend but in this instance I don't trust them. Not after all these seven years I've begged people. I'm a little leery of those who want to show up at the last minute to help me. It's like you know, the devil, and so I just didn't buy into that. September 17th about two o'clock my husband called me and told me that somebody from Channel 1 came out inquiring about me not doing the story. My husband told me he knew nothing about it but he did know that I had contacted Channel 1 in the previous months or years and they ignored my cry. And so that was blown off. At three o'clock on September 17th I was on the radio station. For the first time I had an opportunity to tell my story. The people that violated me, misused me, abused me, raped me, I got a chance to tell the public that this case was built on a major cover-up and how good God has been to me through all of this. I don't care how long it takes in life, never give up. Don't give up. Keep pressing and holding onto God's unchanging hands. And so it was a privilege to talk on KBCO. It was an honor to me that God has just blessed me and told me 'In due time Pamela, I will reveal all things.' And God has stood by His word. His word does not come back void, and I'm standing on His promises. And God through the months has been telling me to call the devils out. And I never understood what He meant and it came to me so clearly when in school the teacher did a roll call. She called your name and you say here, present or raise your hand. Well, God told me to roll call on the enemies. Let these devils be called out. And I called them out from the Attorney General's office to the Lieutenant that hid the glass salt shaker and didn't produce it in the evidence room and didn't have it, he said. The District Attorney, the previous director of DOC, the regional director for DOC. I called these people out because they failed to help me, covered up the case, ignored my cry, did everything they could to shut me down as an inmate who has rights. But God had a different story for them. So I thank God for the radio station that allowed me an opportunity to tell my story. Everything the devil thinks he did for bad to me, God has just turned into nothing but good. And just because the story wasn't told seven years ago, it has not spoiled. So I thank God for that. Thank you Lord. Everyone I begged for justice, all people, especially law enforcement, were a part of the Silent Coalition. FBI and U.S. Justice Department, Tulsa and Washington, DC.

Yesterday a dollar-type store on 41st and Garnett opened the door for me to sit outside. God opened another door. In fact they opened two locations. They said, 'You can sit at two locations to get those signatures. We want to be a help to you.' I thank God for how the people have just in the Tulsa community, east, west, north and south, blacks and whites come together to help Pamela Smith on this case, it's been nobody but God. Nobody but God has been with me. And I thank Him, thank Him, thank Him.

CHAPTER 13

Today is Wednesday, September 22, 2004. It is six o'clock in the morning. I got up to praise God and thank Him for whatever it is He needed me to do today. I've asked Him to just order my footsteps, tell me what He wants me to do. 'And if it sounds crazy to man, I'm willing to do it, God.' I look forward to doing my signatures today. Turning them in and believing in God that every one of those signatures have been ordained by Him. I just thank God that this part of the battle is over. But I know I've got more work to do for God. I don't know what it is that God has for me to do but I'm telling God right now, I'm willing to do it. This is just the beginning of a journey for God and I'm willing to do it. I thank God for 'Neighbor For Neighbor', a lady named Ann and another lady named Nancy. Two white women that I didn't know absolutely anything about, opened the doors of 'Neighbor For Neighbor' for me to get signatures for two days. And I thank God for that. On the last day, which was Tuesday evening, we got relieved about three o'clock, two Christian sisters that had been helping. And they were there Monday and Tuesday and my friend Don Caldwell, who's just like a brother was there. On Tuesday evening, September 21 at three o'clock Theresa said, 'Are we coming back tomorrow?' which would be Wednesday morning, September 22. And I looked at her and I said, 'I don't need to come back. It's already done.' So I thank God for that. But I went out to the store, I guess to release some pressure as telling my story tends to heal me. It may sound strange to people, but telling just brings back pain and bad memories but then I get that out of me. The more I tell it, the better I feel. And sometimes you've got to cry sometimes telling it, but it's okay. All that you're going through, you've got to bear some kind of tears. This is nothing that somebody can zoom through and tell without having some kind of heartaches and pains and flashbacks of something so devastating to them. Such a horrific crime to be imposed upon somebody and then somebody ignores it like this. But I know my God, I know my God. Looking forward to four o'clock today, Candace is supposed to be there with us to turn in the signatures. But I thank God for all these things I ask, that He's granted to me to do. The ability to fight. The willpower. The driving force of Him to help me to keep going with my family and friends. So today is a very rejoiceful day for me. This is the day that my fight begins, my journey for justice will begin, and I thank God for that.

Wednesday morning I got up and was so happy, rejoicing in the Lord that I went down to the election board, walked in and started singing, *This Is The Day That The Lord Has Made*. I was in a good spirit knowing that I have perfect peace in what I've done. I gave it my all and the rest is in God's hands. I turned in some signature cards from registering people to vote at the election board on Denver. The ladies have always been so kind to me there and so I finished that day picking up petitions, signatures and just going around getting the last minute signatures from people. I met with Sharon, Theresa and her sister Mary at a print shop on 51st and Lewis. I was supposed to be there at one o'clock, I got there at five after one, ten after one, and the gentleman had one man waiting on him and another white gentleman came in and I acknowledged who I was. I went to the table and unstapled several sheets of paper which made me be there about one fifteen or one-twenty. So when Theresa and Mary arrived, I told them I had been there and the man hadn't waited on me yet and we tried to figure out how to use the copy machine, so he told us he was going to do it. I looked at Mary and Theresa and I didn't feel this man's spirit. I was not about to let that much power go in somebody's hands, my signatures, be turned over to somebody like that and mess them up. I've come too close. I thank God that He shows me discerning spirits about people. Theresa said, 'Let's go somewhere else' so we discussed where to go. We talked about going to the Print Shop and we decided I'd go to my spot called Office Print where the young lady named Patti had been so kind to me and my brother doing printing. So when we got ready to walk out the door, I told the gentleman, 'Thank you', that I was leaving and he said, 'Okay.' He didn't even try to keep me there or say, well, ma'am give me a few minutes and I'll be with you as a good businessman would do, not wanting to lose a customer. He didn't care, he just said okay. So the other gentleman that walked up that waited on him said, 'Are you coming back?' I said, 'No sir, I've been here since five or ten after one and I have a deadline to get these papers turned in.' He said, 'Okay.' They never tried to stop me. You talk about raciest in this city and on this case. There have been so many racist things that people will not understand. Alson's was real good to me until a white gentleman came in complaining but then yet, another petition was going on a murder case and a white man went to another Alson's store and he was standing there getting signatures and there wasn't a thing said about that. I'll tell you, this has been one case built on a lot of lies, deceitfulness, mistrust, misunderstanding, misrepresented, a lot of blinded justice. It's just been too much unjust justice on this case, too much. So I went to the courthouse, Theresa and Mary and I, met my attorney and Steve White there. The three of us went into the ladies restroom on the first floor at the Tulsa County Courthouse and we had prayer in the ladies restroom on the these petitions and just thanking God for all He's done. And so we know it's done, I know it's done. I knew it was done in heaven. And so I know what God's promised me and I'm standing on those promises. Well, after we got ready to go upstairs, Theresa was looking for her other sister, Sharon, so we went on upstairs and we met Steve White. He was sitting on the second floor waiting on me. So us three gathered again and had prayer, laid hands on the petition and just anointed them with God's word, knowing what God can do. By that time the newsman was in the hall waiting for us to come so he interviewed Steve first then me interviewed. My attorney showed up and we turned the petitions in. Channel 23 filmed that. After filming, they interviewed Mike Smart, my attorney and he did an outstanding job. Just spoke very blunt, very suave dude, just got it together. He's a cool dude and dresses sharp. Anyway, it was a blessed day. Don, Mary, Sharon and Theresa and I got in my car just feeling good knowing it was done. It was a done deal, in Jesus' name it was done. We went and got hamburgers at Brown's and we were trying to rush home to see all of us on the television because they interviewed Mary and Theresa as well. However I missed it at the five o'clock news but I did catch it at nine o'clock. Channel 81 has done a wonderful job carrying my story and so I really give honor to God for allowing them to be the ones that stepped to the plate to help me. I watched me at nine o'clock last night and I was very impressed. Just how God is using me to stand out and speak. And through all of this I'm just hoping that I can be able to teach women to come out. This is the worst rape I believe in Oklahoma history, or in the state's history of any person, inmate or lady or whatever. And to come out and be this strong and this forceful and the driving force on this is nobody but God. Nobody but my Father. And so that was my day, September 22nd, Wednesday, 2004. A blessed day, a blessed day that God allowed us to turn in the petitions. Candace Rowe and her mother showed up at the courthouse but it was too late. They showed up after the interview was over so Candace did not get a chance to do an interview with Channel 23. I was very disappointed in that because I wanted her to always be a part of this. Everything I did, every time I got ready to go on television, I would call up and let her know this is very important to let people see you telling your story, because first of all you've got to come to reality of making up your mind and saying 'I'm going to do this.' I don't care how painful it is. I don't care how degrading it is. I don't care what my friends and family and people think about me. You've got to know where you're going with this and what your focus point is and where you're trying to arrive at with this. And all I ever wanted on this case from day one was justice. And justice for me was making this man and the State be held liable for action this man has inflicted upon me, rape, torture, made me damaged collateral. You don't buy something that's been damaged. And if you do, you look for a discount on it. So I was whole before this man tortured me, raped me and forced me, but I know God is good and the reality part of this, I will probably be scarred for life although I know that God can heal all broken wounds, scars, everything. Your heart can get healed once you have surgery and the doctor cuts on you, you may heal on the inside but that scar is still there. So I still will have a scar for life, no matter what. So I thank God. And that scar I thank God for because that scar reminds me of what God brought me through. Every time I look at that scar, in fact I've got some scars on my body, that I went through some painful things, and every time I look at that scar I remember what I went through to get that scar. I'm healed on the inside but I've still got that scar to remind me not to go that way again. And when you have so much pain inflicted upon you, you just don't forget it. No matter what. And I was raped, tortured and forced by instrumentation and I'll never forget how my sister died in the hospital and I begged this man to let me go say goodbye to her. Such a tragic thing for me. But I know through all of this I have forgiven this man. I do blame the Attorney General himself because he could have stopped this when the little fifteen year old girl made a complaint. They should have looked closely. First of all, she was black, she was poor, she was on the wrong side of town. And so they just figured it was so important to save this man. saying this little girl was spoiled and made that up. But I knew that when this man violated me that God was not going to let me be quiet. He had to use me to rise up to be a voice for other women and other situations that went on in the prison system, so many women being raped and violated in prison. So I thank God that He's using me. I'm on a mighty mission for God and I love serving God. It's been a painful battle but anything God has asked anybody to do, I don't recall was easy. Because if it were easy, God would have called anybody. He picked the ones that He knew that could survive it, could stand the test. Although the test seemed like it was a little hard at times and I wanted to give up but I kept on pressing, kept climbing the rough side of the mountains. And climbing the rough side of the mountains means perseverance. You just hang in there, keep going, don't ever give up. Never give up. No matter what it is in life, keep fighting, keep fighting.

Saturday I called Senator Maxine Horner and asked her if she would call the election board to talk to the lady named Kelly that runs the election board to find out about my signatures. The Senator called and talked to Kelly and was told the signatures looked really good, really good. So I had a sleepless night Saturday night and Sunday night, anxious for Monday morning to call the election board and find out. Monday, September 27, 2004 I got up about quarter to nine and I called the election board. I couldn't hardly take anymore. I called and asked if my signatures were all verified and the lady told me she couldn't tell me that. She said, 'But I can tell you that you got them' meaning she couldn't give me the count or anything but she just wanted to let me know that everything was looking good. So she put Kelly on the phone and I asked her, 'Kelly, can you tell me if I got the signatures?' She said 'I don't want to say anything until the paperwork's all put together but I can tell you it looks better. It looks better than the last time.' So I thanked God for that.

Well, today is Tuesday, September 28th. I got up this morning, took my husband to Oklahoma City to the doctor. Before I went I got a call early in the morning from a lady named Jill, early Tuesday morning about nine thirty, I guess. She called to read my article in the newspaper that I had the total amount of signatures that I received on the Grand Jury Petition. I was so thankful to God when she was reading that to me, my heart fell to my stomach. I just couldn't believe, you know, I know hard work pays off but it was just like all I could do was say thank you God and just sit there and listen to her read that article over the phone to me. After she finished reading that to me, I called everybody I could to tell them. I called my son and I was so excited to tell him that I did it, because my son knows how hard I worked the first time, and how determined his mother is. I hope if nothing else I ever do in life, I taught my son and grandson to fight for what's right in life. When someone misuses you or violates you and you know you're right, don't ever give up. Never give up. Don't ever quit. And so I was so excited telling my son. I was getting ready to take my husband to Oklahoma City to the Veteran's Administration about his eye and Channel 23 called, a man named Jack Steele. He's assignment manager and he called me on one line so I told him I had Julie on, so I went back and told Julie that Jack was on the other line. So Jack told me that he wanted to do a story on me today. I told him I was on my way to Oklahoma City to take my husband to the Veteran's Administration to see about his eye. And I said, 'We can do it tomorrow' which would be Wednesday. He said, 'No, I want to do it today.' I said, 'Well, I'll tell you what, I'm on 51st and Yale if you all want to meet me on 51st and Yale in this area I'll do the story.' He said, 'We can get a person over there to that area' so he dispatched a cameraman out and we met at 51st and Yale at the LaFortune Park and I stood there and did an interview with Channel 23 and my husband sat in the car. I'm so thankful for my husband. I have a good husband, a supportive husband, and I thank God for him. I know this has hurt him mentally and drained him to see his wife hurt like this. But I know that God is going to heal both of our hearts and just mend the pieces back together. But after I did the interview my husband and I went down the highway and I took him onto Oklahoma City to get his eye checked. When I was heading to Oklahoma City I had numerous phone calls, some people calling to congratulate me. Just the devil's always lurking to mess with you when you're getting blessings from God. So I just thank God for all my friends. I talked to Maxine Horner, my brother R.L., Wilbert Collins, my friend, Sirretta, Equita Goodwin, Dee, Connie, gosh, you name them, I talked to them. Just so many friends. People calling and congratulating me, Theresa and, wow, it just goes on and on and on, how people were just so happy for me. I talked to my lawyer, Mike Smart and his secretary, and the appeals attorney. I was just overjoyed today, overjoyed, thankful, just thankful that I know help's on the way, and I believe that in my heart. So no matter how long it takes, never give up. Never give up. Don't ever give up. Press on until you get to the end results of anything. If you give up, you'll never know what the end result was going to be, so I thank God. My husband and I made it back home from Oklahoma City. I came in and changed clothes and I went to Cheap For Less where I cut a commercial for Cheap For Less, thanking the public for supporting me in this Grand Jury Petition. I just want to be grateful to everybody that has come to support me, prayers and everything they sent up. I'm just so grateful to God for it. So I did the commercial for Cheap For Less. After that Steve and I stood and talked and made a couple of phone calls and I headed home. Just so thankful to God. Today has been a blessed day. This has been the day that the Lord has made. I will rejoice and be glad in it. My footsteps in my life have been ordered by nobody but God. Nothing or nobody, what they say, scandalize me, lie about me, it would not stop me from being on the mission I'm on for the Lord and doing what's right. All I'm looking for is justice, true justice. I want to see God prevail so strongly in this case. More than myself. I just want to see how God is, how magnificent He is. How He works through people and how God is just showing himself, revealing himself to me so many times through so many illustrations of this case. It just blows me away. It blows me away.

CHAPTER 14

Wednesday morning I got up, said my prayer and thanked God for what the day was going to bring. My husband and I made preparations to head to the courthouse. We arrived at Tulsa County Courthouse, around nine twenty, nine twenty-five and there was Don and some other people there that I invited to hear the judge grant the signatures to be certified. It was a day to be so grateful to God about. So thankful. Just looking back from where I started and where I'm at today with this case, it's a remarkable blessing from God. So the Judge, Senator Maxine Horner, Representative Jabar Shumate, Don Caldwell, Steve White, my husband Eddie, Candace Rowe, Candace's mother and the grandbaby were all there. Wow, a friend of Don's and my attorney were there from Jones & Jones Law Firm. He said he'd come to support me. Anyway, I was so overjoyed when the Judge said that the signatures are certified, that he set a date for October the 25th. What a rejoicing feeling. What a blessing from God. High at that moment I just couldn't do anything but just raise my hands in the courtroom above my shoulders and say thank you God. I was sitting next to Senator Maxine Horner, holding Candace's hand at one point. But after that I remember just raising my hands and thanking God. Just thanking Him. And looking dead right at the Judge and thinking that this man was a fair judge. You know, it's just something about people, if you've got a good judgement and character of people you can kind of like line your spirit up with people and see what it's going to be like. And with this man, I honestly believe in my heart that he wants justice on this case. He just wants to know himself, how someone could rape and torture and force a lady like this and nobody heard her cry. And I think that God has sent this man to help me. I do believe that. I believe that in my heart, Judge Tim

Grass, and I thank God for him giving me a second chance to do this petition. He could have said no the first time but he didn't. He allowed me to do it again. But I thank God today for everything. My husband has just been faithfully standing by my side, although my husband's not a well man but I thank God for him. He goes along and supports me no matter what. He'll do whatever it takes. The day ended up in a blessed day. I talked to Steve White a couple of times and we were just grateful for what God had done for us and so I went and talked on the radio, made some tapes, commercials for this Saturday coming up for our party, the Thank You party at Cheap For Less.

September the 30th. There was an article in the *Talk World* that the Judge had granted me a court date of October 25th to impanel a Grand Jury. My son Maurice came over and he told me about it, so I went to the store and bought a newspaper to read. I am looking forward to sitting down, talking to a Grand Jury. Believe in God for every word that comes out of my mouth that I'm going to get some justice on this case. I went in before thinking that a jury would do the right thing and I'm asking God to please touch these peoples' hearts to do the right thing today for me on this Grand Jury investigation.

Today is Saturday, October the 2nd. At twelve o'clock today I had a reception from twelve to three. It was filled with so many people, good wishers, congratulated me on my petition drive and getting the signatures I needed to bring in a Grand Jury. Senator Maxine Horner was on hand. A lady named Carla, an outstanding woman, an attorney by the name of Linda, Steve White was there and my friend Don Caldwell, a friend named Willie Colbert, my husband, just a lot of people came back. Candace's grandmother stopped by. A lot of good wishers wishing me on. It was a very good day. After we left there, my husband and I came home. We had a few moments together. I met Linda and Carla at a restaurant called Calbert's. We sat there talked and Linda gave me some advice as far as what to do, how to prepare myself for the Grand Jury. And we talked about my case.

You know, they asked me what I wanted to do when this is all over with and I told them just open up a halfway house and help young ladies to be able to re-integrate with their families, as long as it's built on a Christian foundation, that's what I wanted. They could see other things that I probably wasn't looking for in my own eyes. But whatever it is that God wanted me to do, I'm willing to do it. Any price for God I would do it. I committed myself to wherever God tells me to go, whatever he tells me to say, I will do it. All God's going to require me to do is go and He will speak for me. So I met with those ladies. I spoke with my brother R.L. today. In fact my brother R.L. was at the reception for awhile. Spoke to my girlfriend Johnnie today, a good friend of mine, my best friend, of Grand Prairie, Texas. She was just happy for me and told me I sounded really good. I am happy. Looking forward to going to church tomorrow. Looking forward to giving God all the glory in Jesus' name.

Today is Sunday, October the 3rd. I prepared getting ready for church this morning, gave God His praise. Looking back over my life, everything I've been through, just reassessing and evaluating and just looking back, back down memory lane. Where I am right now today in my life I thank God. I went to the eleven o'clock service at Greater Love Temple. So grateful to God to see Steve White there this morning, a man that truly does love God, seeking to know God. Sat with them. My friend Toni came and sat with me this morning and we just had a good time in the Lord. I went down with Don for prayer. Just such an anointed service from my pastor. I always look forward to serving God.

After church was over we stood outside and talked awhile, Greg and Toni and I, and I ended up giving my pastor and his wife and children a ride home after church. We visited a little bit about what Sister Camilla's going through with her brother that got beaten to death in Wichita, Kansas, and just sharing with them my experience of standing up and fighting and going against everything and what I'm going against right now as far as bringing in my Grand Jury, that I thank God that He allowed me to have and nobody but God did this. And I was sharing with them how hard work does pay off and sometimes when you start a journey you just say, ‘Lord how am I going to see my way through this?’ not knowing that when you enter into that journey God already had the master plan completed but you just have to keep going so you can see that the mission will be completed when you start something. My pastor said some kind things. ‘Sister Pamela, you know they’ve got this Vision 2025. Your case is so strong. It’s just messing up Oklahoma’s image right now.’ And I said, ‘You know what? It’s amazing how God can take an old crack head, an old criminal and all of a sudden I was a nobody to these people that misused me, lied about me, these State officials and all of a sudden God has made me the head and not the tail, and right now I’ve got the power to ask the Grand Jury to call in all of these big highfalutin people with these high big title names. And so it’s just amazing how God can turn things around and use a nothing or someone to turn things around to the glory of Him and I thank God for that. Why did the Attorney General’s office not seek justice for Pamela and Candace?

After I came home I sat and visited with my husband and we talked about everything that was going on and just chilled and had some dinner together. I just thank God, like I said, where I’m at in my life today, I feel good. I will never ever have my life be the same. I’ve gone through so much, more than ten people could endure. I have endured a lot but I know that everything I’ve gone through God knew that Pamela Smith could endure it. He wouldn’t have taken me to it if He didn’t think He could bring me through it. And so I thank God.

Today is October 4, 2004. This morning I got up and went to the Tulsa Federal Courthouse to pickup some documents, to get ready to start putting my file together to get ready for my Grand Jury. I also left there and went and met my brother Eddie at the office to start moving out stuff to close down our business. I have just neglected Blazing Pickles on this case. R.L., my brother, couldn’t make any sales, my mind was so focused on this case to where I was no good in my office and so we just thought it was best to close down for now. After I did that I went and met with Steve White for lunch. He mailed my packets off to *20/20* today to get my story told. We laid hands on them and prayed about it and believed God that that story was going to be aired, that the enemy is not going to get a foothold on this case. All the dirt they think they're doing, we believe in God for exposure on this case. In Jesus' name. After I left there I went to see my lawyer, Mike Smart, and picked up some papers that he had requested from the Freedom Information Act on this case that he never got. I left there and I went to pick up some office supplies to put this portfolio together. Just a very trying day today. After I did that I called Mitt Shaver and asked him if he could possibly get a copy of this report from the District Attorney's office that declined my case in March of 1999. He said he couldn't do it and asked me why I couldn't get another attorney to do it. I have a lot of mixed emotions about my attorneys right now, both of them, Mitt Shaver and Mike Smart. I'm just not feeling these boys at all. Trust just doesn't seem to live in me to trust these men. I don't know if it's just because I test the spirit, I'm not getting a response back from things that I throw out there at them. So disappointed in that and I called Mike Smart's office and his secretary said that Mike Smart said he couldn't get it so I just say well, I'm not going to worry. These devils are not going to stop me from getting the reports I need to get for this Grand Jury. So I moved past that. After I did that I met with a Federal agent today and she talked and gave me a lot of high points today and I thank God for her. Also I met with Diane Stetter today. She pulled some reports off the computer for me about Oklahoma statutes on rape. Also I left there and I went home and just started putting things together in my folder and I just thank God that this day is over with. This has been a very stressful, busy, busy day for me today.

Thursday, October 7, 2004. Letter to 20/20 ABC, I mailed off some correspondence, documents, a video and newspaper clippings and my story and Candace's story to

Oprah Winfrey. I wrote her two letters and Candace wrote her one.

Later on that day around four o'clock I got a call from my attorney, Mike Smart, telling me that the Judge had postponed the date of the Grand Jury impaneling from the 25th of October to November 22, 2004 and the reason why was that you cannot have a Grand Jury going on within thirty days of a major election. I called the Judge's chambers just to confirm it. At this point in my life I don't trust anybody but God. I don't even trust the lawyers that I paid. That's all I did is pay them for bad advice. It is all about money to most attorneys.

After Mike Smart told me that the impaneling of the Grand Jury had been postponed, he went on to say, 'Pamela, I don't think that you should try to draw the conclusion of a conspiracy. You need to just try to focus on the State Drivers Examiner and get an indictment on him.' I was livid. I was mad. I went off on my attorney to let him know that he's only been on my case four months. He was just hired to do the Grand Jury Petition, not to give me advice, and to tell me nothing else. And I paid him seventy-five hundred dollars to do this and so he called to tell me that I shouldn't be trying to show a conspiracy, just focus on the State Drivers Examiner. Well, I told him, not politely, that he doesn't know my case, he doesn't know what's been inside of me for seven years, the hell I've gone through, the people that have played major parts in covering up this case, had never had proper documents and I told him he doesn't know anything, he can't begin to tell this story. I've lived this pain. I've lived these last hours, what these people have done to me, scandalize me, hurt me and violate me and my family. So I went off to tell him that I don't need him to try to protect his friends. He said, 'Well I don't think you need to be trying to show a conspiracy on Diane Small.' Diane Small was the lady that closed my case in the District Attorney's office and why she closed it was, we'll get to that during the jury trial or the Grand Jury and let her come in and tell why she closed it. And I went off on my attorney because I feel like he's trying to cover up for somebody and he doesn't need to be trying to tell me. If he were a good attorney he would say, 'Pamela, you're right. Go in and challenge the conspiracy theory' because this is what this case has been built on. How do you tell that the State Drivers Examiner raped me and there's not a police report if you don't tell this part of the story? So you've got to tell all of it. And if it just so happens that people that should have authority had not done their job, fell short of an indictment, that's not my fault. So I hung up the phone and I called him back and said, 'Mike, don't call me with anything else about my case' and he was like a church house mouse. You couldn't even hear him when I was talking. He's the most negative attorney I every met in my life. And believe me, Pamela Smith has been encountered with a lot of attorneys. This is the most negative attorney. But then I had to search myself and say, Pamela, this man hasn't lived your pain. He has no way to know what you've gone through, so you just press on with what you promised God that you would do and remember that. Remember the struggle. Remember the promises. Remember the hell you've gone through. If you remember all those things, you'll stay focused on what you're supposed to do, so I'd just as soon not talk to him because his life doesn't line up with mine. His spirit most certainly doesn't line up with mine. So we ended on that note. I hung up the phone and I called R.L. I told R.L. what happened and he said, 'Pamela, don't worry about things. God has already got this under control.' That is the most uplifting, spiritual man that I think I've ever met. Even with his downfalls, struggles and his everyday business that he doesn't have money to meet his obligations, he still praises God in the midst of it all. And I found myself thinking that that isn't anything but the devil, the inside of me is so mad because they know that they're at fault and they're running scared. They never felt this black lady could get a Grand Jury. They never thought she'd get five thousand signatures. And then in my conversation to my lawyer, Mike Smart, I said 'You're the same person that didn't believe Pamela Smith could get five thousand signatures. You didn't believe I could do it. And you think I'm going to listen to you telling me not to tell the Grand Jury that this case is based on conspiracy?' He told me not to do it because the Grand Jury would think I'm crazy for going there. Well, I'm going to take my chance. I told him that my whole case has been built on gut feeling and going against the odds. And today that's what I'm going against in that Grand Jury. I'm going against the odds and the odds are standing on the promise of what God told me that He would do through this case. So there it is.

CHAPTER 15

On Friday, October the 8th I went to Stroud, Oklahoma with my brother R.L. and we went down and called on a couple of stores and took a business card and then we came back through Cushing, went to the cemetery, visited all our graves. My mother, brother, sisters, Dad, grandpa, nephews, nieces, just walked the cemetery just looking at our loved ones and looking at so much pain laying in the ground, but thanking God that my brother and I were still living. But as much as I've gone through these last seven years, sometimes I wondered, why me Lord? Why me? But I know there's a purpose for all this that God has me going through this because it's obviously designed to help someone else that's weaker than I, or cannot stand this kind of battle. And God knew that I could. That's the only reason I could understand this, because a part of me has said, girl give up, but the other part of me said, fight, Pamela, fight. And that's the voice I hear from my brother Leon Brannon, telling me all the time, sister, you fight. He told me this before he passed December 13, 2002. He said, 'Sister, you fight.' He told me this when he found out about this case, how I was raped. This man put his penis in my vagina. He shoved his penis in my mouth. Tortured me with a glass salt shaker and just did everything he could to hurt me. Would even hit me on my shoulders. One day I was eating a hot link and he came in, just smashed up my meat just like he could do that, you know, like I was a nothing. But I thank God for where I'm at today in my life. I really do. I'm grateful. I've been through a lot and I know that God is going to sustain and the victory is His. And I believe in my heart that all the State officials and law enforcement, including the FBI and DOS, Tulsa and Washington, DC that ignore my cry, my calling for help, God is going to prevail on this case. I do believe that.

On October 8th I talked to Jill from Channel 23 and she's going to do an update on Candace and me right before we go the Grand Jury, just to see where my thoughts are at, where I'm going, what I expect from the Grand Jury, just hoping the Grand Jury will come in, listen to the facts, subpoena the evidence it takes to land an indictment on this case. So there was a very uplifting conversation with Jill because she's a news reporter and she really has supported me. From a professional standpoint she has tried to be neutral but she's a woman and she knows what it's like to hurt for another woman. She may not know my pain or ever been raped, but just the pain and the suffering that I've gone through, you know, is just more than one person can endure. And so I thank God for Jill that she took the fight to her supervisor and wanted to do this story and it's brought me to this point with the news, because news is informative. It's supposed to inform the public about what is happening. So I thank God for that.

On October the 9th I just sat around the house, chilled, which was peaceful, I didn't do a whole lot. I just stayed around the house. Just chilled.

Sunday I went to church. A very uplifting speaker, a prophet, was in the house from Mississippi. A very uplifting service. I just thank God for the word that is embedded in me that keeps me strong and keeps me focused on doing the right thing. I started planning on Sunday and early Monday, October the 11th, getting ready for the week to come, having guests come to my home on Saturday, October the 16th, getting ready for some political and spiritual and civil rights leader to come and help me, to make sure that I'm covered on all angles. First of all, I know that the promise is walking with God and if God is not in this thing, it will never work and for seven years I've been walking with God. Nobody but God. But anyway, my Sunday church service was beautiful as usual. I always leave the church knowing that I go to receive and I always leave with such an anointed spirit on me of my pastor, an anointed minister, Pastor Greg Wilson. So

Sunday I just came home after church, hung around the house with my husband, had a quite evening, just sitting still.

Monday running around getting paperwork and documents ready, preparing for the Grand Jury on the 22nd of November of 2004. My Monday, my Tuesday just busy, busy this week.

October the 14th my husband was admitted into the hospital for shortness of breath. Seems like the devil keeps throwing things at me, but no matter what the devil throws at me, I just throw it right back because I know that I serve a mighty God and God gives me more strength to endure anything that comes against me. I have made up my mind, no matter what comes against me I will always stay focused and keep the promise that I promised God in this battle against the State and this man that raped, tortured and forced me by instrumentation of a glass salt shaker, just violated me in the worst way he could, and so I know the promise and I know the focus, so no matter what comes at me I will continue to stand. I will lift my hand and I remember to come back to take care of the business that I have to take care of. I cannot let anything stop me from the real focus of this case, and that is making sure that everything is in line with what I need to say to the Grand Jury. So even my husband's being admitted into the hospital, I'm always by his side no matter what. I spent the night with him at the hospital. He had a good night rest. The doctor gave him a sleeping pill. I think it's the first sleeping pill he'd ever taken in his life and he rested very well. The next morning the doctor came in and saw him and I mentioned to the doctor that whatever she had given him, send it home because it certainly made him rest instead of walking the floors. I know my husband is carrying a lot. He's sick. He's had to stand in front of people and say, 'Can you help sign this petition? My wife's been raped.' That's been a lot for a man to say and do and carrying his own sickness as well. You know, it's hard for a man, it would have to bother his pride. It had to. But he loved me enough, unconditionally, that he could stand there and say, 'Could you help my wife? She was raped, and we need signatures.' I think that took a toll on my husband as well. I mean, you know, nobody's iron, nobody is steel. Even if you are steel long enough, you beat it and beat it and beat it, sooner or later it's going to bend.

I got my husband released out of the hospital. We got his prescriptions, I cooked some neck bones and kind of started cleaning up and getting prepared for company I was going to have coming up this Saturday and so we just kind of hung around. Friday night my oldest brother, R.L., we're just really close brothers and sisters. I'm his little sister and he's my big brother, and I'm the only sister he's got left, the other sisters have passed on. I love all my brothers, Jimmy, Kermit and R.L. We lost Leon December the 13th of 2002. What a devastating blow to me but I have three other brothers that I adore. I love them unconditionally no matter what goes on in life they are my brothers and I love them. I don't care what they may do or say about me or what we say about each other as brothers and sisters, we don't always agree and get along, I love them to death. I mean that from the bones in my body, I love my brothers and I thank God for them, each and every one of them. There isn't anything in the world I wouldn't do for them. They need me and if I can get there, I'll be there.

My brother and I sat around. He did laundry, we watched Fox News, which is one of my favorite news stations, Channel 52, CNN and MSNBC. But anyway, we sat around and visited, he did his laundry and left around ten o'clock p.m. I guess.

CHAPTER 16

Saturday, October the 16th, getting prepared for my guests today. I'm expecting my friends, Senator Maxine Horner, the State President of the NAACP, Miller Newman, a Civil Rights Bishop Phil Liggins, another Bishop, Bishop Victor Broom, some lady friends of mine are stopping by, my Pastor and his wife, Pastor Greg Wilson, Willie Mae and Joyce and several other friends, not to mention the most anointing mother that God has allowed to continue to walk the face of the earth will be gracing our presence today. I'm honored to have in my home with my husband and me, just her anointing alone is a blessing. Mother Grace Tucker called earlier today and told my husband that she will be present here. It's just an honor to have this much love coming into my home and I am so grateful to God. I am probably one of the most grateful persons that you would ever meet that came through all the struggles and the mountain climbing, perseverance, trust in God, humbling myself to God. Just believing when I have my back up against the wall, I am just so grateful to have God's people in my presence. It says a lot about God's people to me that when I can line my life with God, He will line the people up that He wants me to walk in the footsteps of righteousness and I just thank God for Mother Tucker, Mother Grace Tucker. A very anointing lady. She used to visit me in prison and would pray for me. And today, seven years later, she's still standing by my side. Like my friend, Maxine Horner. You know, it's just about to bring tears to my eyes. I'm overjoyed with grace, just grace, thanking God for grace and blessing me with wonderful people that love me. I just cannot thank God enough. I praise Him. I love Him and I just give honor to God for redoing my life all over, allowing me to be the woman I am today and knowing who I am in

Christ. I don't say that lightly. I used to be a pistol and I thank God for change, that He made me over. That He created Him in me, and I love today, I desire today, I feel today. I obey God. I just, I'm just, just happy to be the Pamela Smith I am today, a child of God. One that I know is living for God in her heart. I line my life up to please God, not man. And I just thank Him for all the people again that He has placed in my life. And today, October the 16th will be a blessed day in the Lord. My home will be anointed with so many Christian people, Bishops and Mothers, Mother Tucker, Joyce, another prayer warrior, just so many Christian friends and I thank God for each and every one of them that will be in my home today sharing their support in this Grand Jury Petition for me, and Candace and I thank God for it.

Today has been a blessed day. My guests started arriving at about a quarter to four. It was just truly a blessing today. Everybody I invited with the exception of one person showed up. It was just a privilege to have all these people in my home today. With so much anointing and the blood of the lamb. Steve White that owned Cheap For Less was here also. I guess my neighbors thought, my God what's going on at that lady's house? Has there been a death or something? because I normally don't have that much company, only during the holidays, children, nieces and nephews come and go, but I just was blessed today. The first thing in order was the prayer that we prayed. Sister Joyce prayed for us in the circle where we held hands and prayed. It was such a blessing, it was anointing. Jabar Shumate was here, the young gentleman who's running for State Representative. Willie Mae Colbert was here, a good friend, an older lady. It was just wonderful. A white friend of mine named Lynn Powell. She's over the Oklahoma Cure for Inmates. It was just a blessed feeling. My son, Maurice and grandson Kyante stopped by and it was just a blessing for them to stop in. My older brother R.L. was here but only for a few minutes. He had a date so he left. Candace's mother and grandmother were here, and later Candace joined us and it was just a good feeling. We sat around, ate, laughed, visited with one another and everybody was getting me ready for the Grand Jury, telling me, Pamela, now you've been fighting for seven years. you have been the prosecutor and so now it's time for me to really sit back and prosecute this case and let these other people sit in the seat. And it just made me feel good to hear Maxine say, 'Pamela, you can chill now. You know the Grand Jury's here. You've worked hard for that.' And you know, I want Candace to get so much recognition too because she was young, didn't know which way to go, what to do. Her mother and grandmother didn't know and just because the grace of God allowed me to be able to put her name on the Petition for the Grand Jury. There's nothing but a police report that she filed in the court but they didn't have money and they just didn't know. Everybody doesn't know the law and when you don't know the law or don't know your rights or don't understand the system, you don't know how to work it and so, therefore, you get caught up in it or you get left behind. I thank God that He just gave me knowledge and ability to fight and stand and when I don't know anything or if I don't understand something, I simply ask or say I don't understand that. So I thank God that He allowed me to help Candace to get some justice for herself. You know, she was just a child when this man solicited sex from her for a written test at the driver's license agency. So you know, it's just, a lot of things have come out of this. You know, Bishop Smith asked me in the meeting, '"Surely you're going to write a book?"' I couldn't help but to say yes. How can I not write a book for all this injustice that has taken place in my life? You know, State officials hiding evidence and making it be known that they took the glass salt shaker and put it in a desk drawer. I mean it's just like I don't count. I don't mean anything. You don't take evidence and put it in a desk drawer. You turn it into the property room. So I guess I just thank God for so much that's happened on this case. We had a long visit, I prepared plates for everybody to take food home and thanked God we had so much fun here today. I feel so uplifted that I've got people that love me that were here today in support to help Pamela Smith. And I thank God for that.

So, Mother Tucker was here. She gave me a lot of wisdom. Always has given me knowledge. Mother Grace Tucker used to visit me when I was in prison and pray for me. And then to have her in my home was just more than an honor. I mean, you know, this is the anointing lady, the mother, the queen, the woman that I know God chose. She earned that spot. She told me tonight she had been saved for sixty years. You know that's a long walk with God and to be faithful. And I just hope my life could be inspired by her touch of life that she has and placed upon me. Even when I was in prison I admired her walk and said Lord I'd like to be like her someday, be able to touch people and anoint and just, you could just feel it all in your body and to hear this lady talk. She doesn't speak above a whisper. And everything she says is good, she doesn't gossip. She quotes scriptures and she loves God and she demonstrates it by teaching the word to people and living it herself. She's been a great inspiration to me.

My Pastor called today, Pastor Greg Wilson, and said that he couldn't make it, he had to work but I was grateful for God for that, that he did want to be a part of this. But I just had a blessed day today. I thank God. My house is so anointed. I'll sleep like a queen tonight. And I thank God, I thank God, nobody but God has done this. And I'm looking forward to November the 22nd. If life lasts and time passes and God permits me to sit before the Grand Jury, I will tell them everything that they need to know. As the songwriter's song, *Go Tell It On the Mountain,* I'm going to tell it on the mountains, and all things in Jesus' name. I will be obedient to the word of God. I just love God. He's been good to me and I just thank Him for this day, October 16, 2004. A blessed day.

I told a group of people today that I came out of prison without a prison jacket. Your jacket is supposed to follow you wherever you go and I do not have a jacket. And I told them that on October the 7th, the probation lady told me she could never find my jacket. They had to create a jacket on me and that tells me that this case has been nothing but a major cover up. But, you know, what man think he's done to hurt me, I know God sees all things, and I know in due time, I know what God promised me. I don't care how dim it looked, how bad it looked, I don't care how the lawyers say do this or do that, I am following God on this case. I'm doing what God said to do. Lawyers gave me advice and my spirit doesn't line up with it and I don't do what they say. I'm going with God. I'm going with God whose been with me for seven years on this case when I didn't have any lawyers. I didn't have anybody to give me advice and tell me what to do and what to say. I backed up against the wall, fell on my knees in a cold cell on a cement floor, out of the steel bed at one or two o'clock in the morning praying, nobody but God and me. I'm crying, laying on that flat mattress in the cell crying out to God, stretching my hands to Thee, asking God to help me deliver me from this. And how I would stand if He would just show me what to do through this case. And He showed me. There isn't any way in the world I would listen to man over God in this case. There's no way. Absolutely no way. And so I thank God for being my Father.

Today is Monday, October the 18th. I got up this morning and read a story about a black guy being sexually abused, a slavery story, in the prison, being raped. It was given to me by a lady named Louise Pete. I got up and read the article and I found out the reporter's name. God gave me favor. I dialed that number and that reporter answered that phone. That is so unusual. He gave me his fax number and I faxed some documents to him about my story. Just believe in God that my story's going to finally get some attention to it and I thank God for that. It's finally getting the attention it deserves. It should have been told many years ago but because of all the stale fishes involved and doing the things that they have done on this case, it never got told.

I'm getting prepared to go to the doctor today. I've been having some shortness of breath, just been so focused on this case that I'm really run down. And I'm sure the doctor's probably going to admit me into the hospital for some rest and to get away from everything, and so I'm going today to just see. I'm a fighter. I'm still strong. My constitution is strong. I will not give up. I don't know what the problem may be but I'm not surrendering to it because I'm looking forward to November 22, 2004. The day that I get to hear that a Grand Jury will be impaneled for Pamela Smith. This has been a long fight for me. And so my husband is getting prepared to take me to the doctor today. I saw my brother, R.L., today.

Let me back up a little bit. My only grandson, Kyante, and Maurice came over yesterday, Sunday, October the 17th. Kyante laid in the bed with grandma and watched some movies and I just fell asleep knowing I had my little precious pride and joy with me.

Now going back to Monday, October the 18th. This is the day that my transcripts are supposed to be ready and I'm looking forward to that. The court reporter is supposed to have them ready to give to the attorney's, Jones & Jones. Also, the lady from the court reporter that did the deposition on the State Drivers Examiner and his supervisor called me today to let me know that she can get a copy of them to me and I'm thankful for that. So I will be picking up a copy of those depositions also. I'm not nervous, I'm not afraid, I'm just ready. You know, when you've got the truth in you, you don't let anybody frighten you or intimidate you, under no circumstances. So, that's where I'm at today. Right now it's twelve thirty-seven on Monday, October 18, 2004.

I went to the doctor at one-thirty today and told him about my chest pains and being numb and a few other things. So he's going to see me on Friday to have a test done to shoot dye up to my heart to see if I've got any arteries closed. But I believe in God that I'm going to be fine, just maybe a lot of stress from working on this case. So about six o'clock this evening I called and talked to my attorney with Jones & Jones Law Firm and I had asked him to make sure they get my transcript ready because I need it. He said that the court reporter did not call back today to let him know that she had it ready. I told him I need it because there's things I need in it and there's some things said in the courtroom that Candace needs to know as well. So anyway, they said that they would have it. He would try to call the court reporter or she should be calling him tomorrow to let him know they got it. Another thing he said to me, 'Be careful about letting letters go out that we send you that have confidential information in them.' Well, I told him it's a little bit too late because I had already released the letters to my friend and that he had already sent the letters to the press. So he was really concerned about that and I discussed with him that I don't see how Mr. Hall could say that my case was very weak because he hasn't even seen the transcript. The transcript is what you look at to make your appeals to Denver, and you look to correct things on that transcript that will help you to send your appeals onto Denver. In the beginning the appeals attorney told me that Leroy Hall's a good attorney, that he has a good rapport with the 10th Circuit Court of Appeals, that his ruling are respected because he doesn't just send anything up there and he's respected by the 10th Circuit Court of Appeal and gave me all this good song and dance about Leroy Hall, how good he was. Well then I get this letter September, I believe the 18th, telling me that Mr. Hall is not sure how it's going to turn out in Denver because of ninety-nine percent or ninety percent of juries are not turned over. That all may be true, but until you've got a transcript in front of you, you cannot really assess an appeal until you look at the errors that were grossly done wrong in a courtroom. And so you may not turn over a jury's ruling, and I'm not going to say you can't, because anything's possible with God, but there could be gross mistakes done that went on in that courtroom and so that's why I challenge that and I think that they were concerned that I let that letter get out of my hands and into other people's possession simply because of that. I got off the phone and I laughed because it kind of let me know that who's zooming who again and what people really stand on issues in my life and who’s really been truthful about everything. I called my brother to tell him so we could get a good laugh today.

CHAPTER 17

Today is October the 20th. Today I talked to my attorney, Mike Smart, and asked him if they had picked the advisor for the Grand Jury that's going to convene on the 22nd of November. He said not as of yet but he will call the judge to find out. I told him not to hurry, but as soon as he finds out something to let me know who the attorney's going to be representing me on this Grand Jury Petition of Investigation. I talked to my brother R.L. this morning. He brought a roast over for me to cook for him and us to have for supper this evening. That was about ten thirty this morning. About ten forty-five this morning I talked to Carolyn and she had typed up a letter, got it ready for me to get to the FBI. Also, I talked to Esther Vaughn today and just went over some personal things with her. I then helped prepare letters to Mr. Miller Newman, Senator Maxine Horner, Aldon Little with the *No Your Tell*, Jill Clark with Channel 23 and faxed a letter to Niki with the ACLU in Washington DC There was a letter that I was getting ready to mail to Mr. Duke Kilgore of the FBI, informing him that I have been home going on five years and I still do not have a field jacket at DOC

Probation and Parole at 440 South Houston. I'm getting ready right now to go downtown. It's two o'nine. I'm going to see Mary Cobb to see what she can tell me about why I do not have a field jacket and out on parole. And also, how they're able to assess me, audit my books, count me as a State inmate, whatever they need to do, how do they process it if my jacket cannot be located at the probation and parole office? I have literally had to build my own jacket. Miss Kathy Laws, a lady named Denise I used to have, and also Ms. Mary Cobb. We have had to just go from scratch. I've had to tell them that I owe probation in Stillwater. I owe money here and this is how much time I've got. They had no clue whatsoever, so I'm getting ready to see Mary Cobb to see if I can get some kind of answers and get a copy of my receipt where I paid this $600 in November of 2000, that somehow a charge came up after I was home one month or two.

At three fifteen today I met with Mary Cobb, my parole supervisor. We sat down and went over documents. I asked her about the receipt in paying the bill that I paid back in November of 2000, or December when I came home from prison. I also told her that I needed her to write me a letter so I can have it when I go before the Grand Jury to say how well I've done since I've been on parole. Also, I asked her if there was anyway possible for a person to come out of prison without their field file? She said no. She told me that normally a file will show up a month or two later, maybe three months or so, but not this long. I said, 'What, five years?' and she said, 'No, this is unusual.' So she got on the computer and looked to see if she could locate the file somewhere else and the computer data showed that it was not there. And I said, 'Well didn't Ms. Lilly Dawes tell you last week or a couple of weeks ago that legal had it in Oklahoma City?' She nodded her head and said, 'Yes.' She said, 'Pamela, this is all I have from September 8, 2000 until today. This is what you call the parole jacket. You need your field file while you were in the institution and we have none of that. Absolutely none.' So she wrote down all the information of what I needed to have subpoenaed to get my medical records, my institutional records from DOC. So I left there. My brother called while I was in the meeting and we talked for a few minutes and visited and I went home and just prepared this notation to get it ready to be typed.

Today is Thursday, October the 21st. Today Oklahoma Cure President Lynn Powell called to let me know that there was an article in the newspaper, the *Talk World*, about a Sheriff having sex with inmates. And in that article it stated that inmates are incapable of consenting to anything. We do not have the voice and authority to do that because we are warded to the State and in the custody of someone with supervision over us. I got a copy of that article. My brother came by and we went to the Hot Dogs To Go, sat there and ate, then I bought two newspapers and took them home and read the article. My husband read the article and he just said that man is a goner. I said, 'Well, looks like he and the State Drivers Examiner are going to be sharing the cell together violating those young ladies like that. I mean, this stuff has got to stop.' Also I put a call into the FBI just to check and see, just touch base with them. I'm leaning on God but God also puts people in your path that He knows are going to direct you and give you good advice, not send you into a tailspin like the State has been trying to do to me for seven years, but I just refuse to go away. And that's because of the force of God that lives in me. Also about four o'clock today I called the FBI and asked to speak to Mr. Phil Kilgore. He was not in and the secretary took my name and number. I've written them several letters begging them to help me on this case. Back in January 2004 one of the FBI agents stated that she couldn't help me, that they couldn't help because I lost in a civil case. I don't think that's grounds to close any case. My civil rights have been violated. There's never been a police report on this case. There's never been any of my rights read to me on this case. The only time my rights were read was after I did a polygraph the second time. They took it into the District Attorney's office to try to enhance somebody to make a decision on closing this case. I have met with the FBI, Tulsa, Oklahoma City and Washington, DC No help. Also there's never been a DNA done on me. Absolutely none whatsoever. I've never talked to a Tulsa Police and I was raped in Tulsa County in a DPS building, a State agency building in a storage room on 36th Street North, 575 East 36th Street North. So I was just calling today to see what kind of assistance can I get from the FBI to help me make sure that this man is prosecuted and the people that broke the law and State officials in a capacity that tried to cover up evidence on this case, so I wanted to talk to the FBI today to just follow-up on that.

Also I just had a blessed today. I mailed the letter off today to Kermit, my little baby brother that was in jail. I want him to learn his lesson and get out of jail. I mailed him a letter and some pictures today, just letting him know that I love him. That his sister wants him to do well, come out of there and let that be a lesson learned, not to return to jail. He can't continue to wobble in the same mistakes and think that it won't ever get better. Make a mistake, learn from it, get over it, move on with your life. And don't look back, just keep going forward.

Today is Saturday, October 23rd. Around one forty-five, two o'clock, Steve White and I went to Tellie's location at a body shop where he was working and gave a statement on tape that the State Drivers Examiner had purchased condoms from him before. And other guys had and so today I thank God that we got that down. Now he told us that he would give us a written statement as well to tell that the State Drivers Examiner did purchase condemns from him and he gave this with no obligations other than ask to come in and tell nothing but the truth. Nothing but the truth on this case. Whatever it is, tell it. If the State Drivers Examiner bought condemns during the time Pamela Smith worked at DPS seven years ago, just tell it. Yes, I thank God for that.

Also I got my transcript copy today. I went to Jones & Jones and picked it up, got copies, took the original transcript right back down to Jones & Jones. The lady was there that checked them out to me and the same lady was there when I went in and got them copied. And I thank God I got that achieved today. So I got a lot of things done today and I thank God for it. Took some pictures at Cheap For Less today and at the Good Citizen Flea Market where I got my signatures.

CHAPTER 18

Today is November 2, 2004. Around one o'clock I talked to the District Attorney in Rogers County and Claremore County. We talked about the case, what to expect of the Grand Jury, that he did not represent me, Candace, or the State Drivers Examiner, he was just going to be the advisor to the Grand Jury, to lay down the rules. I had an interesting conversation with him. I felt uneasy about it, found some discomfort in talking to him, that I'm not worried about somebody going up and keeping me from telling the Grand Jury the story. Also I spoke with my attorney, Mike Smart, about the Grand Jury. We talked about Candace's mother's and grandmother's letter that they wrote off to the Judge. Mike Smart said he never received his, so what I did was I faxed him a copy of it. I met with my attorney and took him a copy of the letter, face to face, putting him on notice about it and letting him know that Candace and I had written the judge. Also I went by and talked to Candace's mother and asked her to please notify the press of this information that they have on this case, to let the press be aware of it and put them on notice that the Supervisor testified in a civil case that he interviewed all three of these people and never did. I faxed John with the *Weekly Oklahoman* in Oklahoma City Candace's letters to the FBI and the supervisor's transcript stating that he never interviewed these people and my letter about the story the *Okie Claw* did on me, my story and Candace's story that she had written to Oprah. I also faxed the Grand Jury Petition with Candace's and my names on it and that's basically all today. My brother R.L. came by to eat supper with us and my brother, Kermit, who's been staying with us, trying to get on his feet as he just got out of jail. I'm so tired and worn out with my own problems but I just asked God to give me strength to help my family when they need a safe haven that I hoped my home could be that because of the love and the anointing that God has blessed upon me, to have in my home. And I thank God for that. Also today I took Kermit to see about a car in Sand Springs. I'm just looking forward to a blessed day. Talked to my son, Maurice and grandson Kyante this evening, around five thirty. Just been a blessed day, a blessed day.

Today is November 4, 2004. This morning around eight thirty my brother Kermit, my husband, Eddie, and I, drove up to Claremore, Oklahoma to meet with the District Attorney up there. I went in the back and talked to him and I picked up some papers that he gave me, where Donna Butt and Gary Rich had declined this case in March of 1999. After I left there I went by and saw Dr. Sneed and got my medical records and put them in my file. I took my husband, Eddie, to the eye doctor and then just hung around the house with Eddie. I made a call to check on his trucking company in Dallas. I talked to Stephanie Als today. She's an attorney that used to work in a District Attorney's office and she told me Donna Butt got a new last name so we visited today about when she worked in the District Attorney's office when my case came in and got declined. I took my brother, Kermit, to his boss so he could work in Muskogee. I stopped by on 11th and Garnett and saw my older brother R.L.. He was out doing his steam cleaning and he needed an extra one hundred foot hose and Eddie and I picked one up for him and took it back to him. And we stopped at Braum's and got us some ice cream, then headed on home.

Friday, November the 5th I believe, Candace Rowe, Steve White and I did an interview at the radio station KCFO 1170 am. It was a great interview, a lot of things were discussed. Also I prepared some documents for the Claremore District Attorney so he could try to get documents for Candace and me for this Grand Jury, i.e. our police reports. I want to go in prepared with all the documents we need. I have to call them Saturday.

My son called and told me my two nephews got

arrested in Enid. Just a typical family problem I guess, but everybody's families have problems. You can't go through life without some ups and downs. So I made a phone call to a bondsman to see if they could try and get those boys out of jail. Two good little young boys. Everybody makes mistakes, and because you make a mistake doesn't make you a bad person. I fix my mistakes in life and try to be an example for them. Other than that, getting prepared to go to church on Sunday morning. I've given God the glory for my wonderful week that He had blessed me to have. I just thank God for my life, my family, my health and my strength. Things I don't have I thank God for.

I'm faxing the Claremore District Attorney a letter requesting the police report for Pamela Smith that was made by Sergeant T. Evans and the police report that was done by the Tulsa Police Department on Candace Rowe. I also requested any recent allegations on the State Drivers Examiner by the District Attorney in Claremore as well. I called his office around eight forty-three this morning and asked for the fax number and the secretary gave it to me, and said that she would make sure he got it. She asked me how many pages it was and I told her I was only faxing one page. On the letter it told the District Attorney that I would be following up with a call to see when I could pick up the documents I had requested.

On November the 8th around ten thirty, eleven o'clock, I put a call in to Mike Smart and said that I needed to speak with him because I had some good news. I had spoken to the FBI earlier that day and he had told me about Lieutenant George Tall knowing about my case from 1999 because he was the OHP trooper that did the polygraph for me. So I called Mike Smart back around eleven forty and told him about that and also George Tall told FBI agent Bobby Wills that he knew I was telling the truth on this case.

Today is November 11, 2004. I mailed letters to Mr. Newman, to Candace Rowe, to other people, George Tay, on this letter that I prepared for Mike Smart asking him to refund my money, dispense my money back to me since he decided that if I go up against his friend, Donna Butt, for an indictment he would get off my case. I prepared letters for the FBI, Mr. Phil Kilgore and Mr. Dennis Mack. Also, I prepared a letter to the District Attorney advisor on the case for Candace and I. I also prepared a letter to other FBI agents on this case and to Mike Smart and Gary Jones of Jones Law Firm, which Mike Smart works at. Also I prepared a letter today of a statement that an attorney gave me down in front of the courthouse the second week of September of 2004, telling me that Donna Butt was the one to close the case and questioned why would the case be closed with these type of charges and Donna Butt responds telling her to just leave it alone, just leave it alone, ignore it.

CHAPTER 19

September 1st, 2nd and 3rd, 2006. The Brannons had their second annual family reunion in Cushing, Oklahoma. All the family members came home. There was a rejoicing time. We had family that came from as far as Chicago, Washington, DC, Kansas City, and Memphis, Tennessee. It was certainly a blessed time in the Lord. Also, we mourned for our loved one that was murdered, shot down by a white landlord in Stillwater. Darren Keith Brannon was shot down and murdered by a white man that just didn't like black people, and we marched for Darren because the police department blocked off the streets, showed the Brannon family loyalty. We marched in song, Martin Luther King's Hymn, holding hands, holding his signs, we had a big press release to the media, just a wonderful time that we had at our family reunion. We also attended Sunday morning services at Mt. Olive Baptist Church, had our Sunday dinner, a memorial dinner, and we just had a joyous time in the Lord. Had a wonderful grandfather, Ray Brannon, which was the first black police officer in Cushing, Oklahoma. He helped my mother raise all eight of his grandchildren. We fought hard to get a street named after my grandfather called Ray Brannon Boulevard. He put his life on the line for many people in Cushing so we thought that it would be a great occasion for him to have a street named after him. I met with the city officials in Cushing three or four months prior to our family reunion and the Board of the Chamber of Commerce decided to vote to honor a man who put his life on the line so other people in Cushing, Payne County, would have a peaceful city to live in. And I thought it was a great honor for my grandfather, to honor him for a job well done by my grandfather. I spoke on behalf of my grandfather at the city town hall meeting in Cushing and it was a pleasure to speak on his behalf, for all the work that he had done for my sisters and brothers, just being a great granddad who looked out for us, taught us so much, instilled so much in us. So I salute my grandfather, Ray Brannon.

January 2006. I went to a meeting that the NAACP State host, Mr. Roosevelt Milton. I was invited to come and share the information about my nephew, Darren, that had been murdered. The audience was just shocked, couldn't believe that a man would lose his life over $350 rent, when in truth it was only $50. So I met the legal redress team, I met James Carpenter and Clarence Powers. They've been a blessing to me, along with the NAACP chapter in Oklahoma City, standing by my side. After begging so many people to help me on this rape case, so many State officials, powerful people, and everybody just did the silent conspiracy to ignore my cry for justice. But I thank God that He sent me James Carpenter and Clarence Powers. They took this case by the head and just got busy, looking into it, reading documents, not believing what they had heard. However, in January 2006, James Carpenter told me that my case was not unique because in 1979 there were other female inmates that had been abused by DPS employees and nothing had been done, that these young ladies had cried out to the ACLU. I myself had cried out to the ACLU back in 1998, asking them to help me and no one would. And so I thank God that the NAACP chapter in Oklahoma City got involved to see that there was justice done for Candace, me and many other girls that were abused sexually, raped, or just simply abused for a drivers license or were powerless over their situation in the hands of this State Drivers Examiner. Our Oklahoma Justice System is broken, especially when it comes to blacks.

After I met up with the NAACP we began to get busy, writing letters to the governor, having press conferences, setting up trying to see if we could get some kind of answers to this case. How does an inmate work in a DPS, even if she is a former inmate, or was an inmate at that time, how do young girls go to get a drivers permit or even want to take a driving test and be solicited for sex. It didn't set good in the NAACP's mind so they got involved, started having press conferences and moving forward on things, trying to get charges filed on this man.

In February of 2006 the NAACP in Tulsa hosted a press conference for Pamela Smith and Candace Rowe. It was about the DPS abusing their power but so very little press showed up. We as blacks do not see press as often as if this were a white girl that had been raped and abused by a black man. Press is not equally fair to us and so only one reporter showed up, and when he did show up, he did air Candace's and my stories. We knew that we were dealing with giants, but both of us are Christian people, we know our foundation and we know who our God is and we know what God can do, and it's been a battle for me for many years. So at that point we continued to do our press conferences and very little press would ever show up for us. We knew that we were fighting the Attorney General's office and we knew that we were black, some of us were poor, most of us had a past, so we knew that there was a lot to overcome. But we continued to trust God, kept going, kept hoping that the wheels of justice would turn for us. So we continued to do what we needed to do to try to see some justice on this case (42 USC 1983 Civil Rights).

On February 4, 2006, Candace Rowe stood up as a brave, young lady, a beautiful young girl, and told her story, a very painful story, how the State Drivers Examiner had taken her into the back room, locked the door and asked her for sex, at fifteen and a half years of age and how it just rocked her world, how it had devastated her and that the state officials promised her, with written letters, that they were going to do something about it. That was in 1998 and nothing has been done for that child at this point, nothing but a bunch of broken promises and a bunch of lies, covering up of a case, designed by the DPS. She has not seen any justice. The only justice she was able to see was when I made her a part of the Grand Jury Petition, to have her name put on it, to get out and get signatures so her voice could be heard at a Grand Jury. The Grand Jury was a joke. November 2004 they mistreated us in the Grand Jury, they would not take Candace's witness list, never called my witnesses, and I had sixty-five witnesses on the list including a doctor that diagnosed me with post-traumatic stress disorder. But I had no witnesses called. They called several of my witnesses on the telephone to talk to them instead of calling them in the courtroom to speak to them in person. So we will continue to be violated on this case. But we continued to press on.

Going back to 2006, we continued to have more press conferences, going to Oklahoma City, having meetings, trying to meet with the governor of Oklahoma or whoever we had to meet with to try to get some kind of justice. Why this man had never had any criminal charges placed on him, when in 1997 he asked Candace Rowe for sex in exchange for a drivers permit, two weeks later he rapes me, inmate Pamela Smith and tortures her with a glass salt shaker, repeatedly rapes her, who then goes to many of the DPS employees at 36th Street North in Tulsa, shows Wayne Wright the condom that the man gave her to rape her with. He laughed, thought it was a joke. He went to the State Drivers Examiner's immediate supervisor and told him and he thought it was a joke and couldn't believe anybody would do something like that. He even made a statement, 'What's wrong with that man? He must be sick.' So nothing was ever done there. We continued to press on, do whatever was necessary for us to do. I've spoken to so many people, continued to make phone calls, continued to fax, continue to write letters, but all my cries, all my <u>begging</u>, all my pleading continued to fall on deaf ears. But even in the midst of all of this, I continue to remain faithful to God because I recall the year 1998. I promised God that I would see this case through. He didn't promise me it was going to be easy. He never promised me that. Everybody God has ever called to do something, I recall has never been easy to do, has always been a task. But I know one thing. God didn't bring me this far to leave me now. And I know that every door that man has shut in my face, God has opened more windows than I can jump out of and He poured me blessings. So today

I never count anything but my blessings. I count blessings more than I do anything and I thank God for where I'm at on this case today because this case has not just been about Pamela Smith or Candace Rowe, it's been about so many female inmates that are raped in prison, have no voice, they make these women be silent of their own abuse. And I promised God that I would fight, no matter if it cost me my life, whatever it cost me, I would continue to fight. And I don't believe that the Lord will allow me to go through this journey if He didn't have a purpose for me to do the work that He calls me to do on this case. There's been times that I feel like giving up, but I've had to remember the promise that I made to God back in 1998, that He would get the glory and I will see justice for the things that the State officials, the State Drivers Examiner, the man that raped me, and all the abuse that goes on around the world in the prison system – female offenders being abused, raped, tortured and then threatened that if they talk they'd be thrown on lock, they'd be pulled from visiting their families, they couldn't go to the canteen (the canteen is where you can go purchase pop and candy, etc.). So to be raped and abused in prison, it is a silent treatment that the State has allowed these prison guards, these jailers, these security guards and these DPS workers, all of these people had the power and it seemed like the State and the courts protect these men rather than trying to look for justice for these female offenders and helping women that have been abused. So I continue to fight on this journey. I promised the Lord that I would continue to move forward, and no matter how many doors close, I keep on going until the Lord tells me it's over. And as of January, February, March, April, May, June and July 2007, I'm still in the storm. I've been fighting this case for many years, but I'm still in the battle.

My rape started in November of 1997, went all the way up until May 1998. But the case was not filed until January of 2000. The civil part of it was filed in January 2000. However, in 1998 and 1999 I begged the DPS, I begged the Governor of Oklahoma, I wrote letters to him, I begged District Attorney, many of these people to help me. I've written many television stations to expose it, to no avail. I was in EWCC at the time that I was trying to seek out the help, but I was raped at the DPS in Tulsa, Oklahoma. I was at a work release center at TCC. I would go out every day to do assignments, clean, janitorial work for the DPS on 36th Street North as well as Jenks, Oklahoma. All of my abuse mainly took place at the DPS on 36th Street North's storage room.

March of 2006 I started hosting the Pamela Smith Rape Foundation, having town hall meetings for people to come together to discuss the issues of prison abuse. At one point we had a Senator Judy McIntyre that had signed a bill that was a very disturbing bill. It was House Bill 2966 and in that bill the language was so damaging to people, especially minority people, because if you look at the statistics today, the prisons are over-filled with minority people, 2.4 million inmates. House Bill 2966 stated that if you were an inmate and if you suffered any kind of abuse while you were in prison, if you didn't file your petition or grievance while you were in prison, when you got out of prison you couldn't sue the state. So that bill was a very disturbing bill because it allowed inmates to be silenced about their own abuse while they were in prison, that they had to be quiet and take that. So when they got out of prison, because they were afraid to file it while they were in prison for fear of becoming a target of abuse. Their time had expired by the time they got out. So we challenged Senator McIntyre from North Tulsa, a black Senator. She came to the town hall meeting and she stated that she didn't know what she signed and she just signed it, which we didn't understand that because you don't sign things you don't read, and being a Senator, although we know that a lot of bills get pushed in front of them, but I think that's nothing but a cop-out to sell out people to say that 'I didn't know what I was signing'. So therefore, it outraged the audience and they had questions for her, but she apologized for it. We went to many ministers, asking them to help us to try to get this bill overturned and nothing was done. The ministers seemed like they could never come together on the same page here in Tulsa to help with unity. When things like this are put before our people to harm our people, and this is a terrible bill, House Bill 2966. It's a nightmare for anybody's family if they've got someone locked up and they've been abused in there. So we couldn't get any cooperation from the black ministers, very few, very few. I did challenge the Attorney General to overturn the bill. No luck.

We moved on. I went to the attorney with the law firm of Jones & Jones and asked him if he would write an opinion. He wrote an opinion and he stated in his letter that the Bill was unconstitutional, what he could see. So then I needed Lee Morris to write an opinion on the Bill. He is a senator in Oklahoma City and also, as well as asking him to write an opinion, get the Attorney General to write an opinion. That fell on deaf ears. So the Bill was out there to where the state had the power to silence and abuse these inmates in the State of Oklahoma. Also as well I'd like to mention that myself, the NAACP, along with my husband, had a meeting with Lee Morris and he brought in a black attorney named Dell. This was in the month of April or May of 2006. We went and met with Lee Morris and he was going to try to help me. The purpose of the meeting was to see if we could get a judicial hearing on the state officials because I felt like they had personally abused their power on the rape case and we were trying to get an investigative hearing and Lee Morris said there was nothing he could do because the case was at the 10th Circuit Court of Appeal, which is a bunch of baloney. He used a black guy to try to cool us down and make it seem like it's real because it's coming out of a black man's mouth, because he had a tendency to think a black person would believe another black person quicker than they would a white person. But that doesn't always work, so we didn't fear Lee Morris and we didn't fear Dell because we knew it was a bunch of baloney, that this man had the state power to ask for an investigative hearing on state officials, their abuse and their power, so that didn't happen.

May of 2006 I went to the cemetery to visit my loved ones. My mother, all three of my sisters, Elweeder, Esther and Diana, my brother Leon, my grandfather Ray Brannon, my father, Raymond Brannon, my nephew Darren, two of my nieces and other relatives and friends. I feel comforted when I go to the cemetery and visit my family because I just feel peace there that I know that that's where their remains are at and I feel comfortable just leaning down to them because I know that whenever I go to the cemetery and visit with my family and cry out to them, it stays there. Just like talking to them as well as talking to the Lord at the same time.

After the cemetery visit I visited some relatives in Cushing. I love going home. It's a small town and I'm just a small town country girl. I had big dreams and still have big dreams. But most of all I am a child of God, I follow the Lord, I let Him guard my footsteps in everything I do. A great joy to have come from a family of eight. My father walked off and left my mom with eight kids and R.L., my oldest brother along with my sister Elweeder, stepped in and saw about their siblings and did a wonderful job. I thank God for them.

The 21st of May 2006. My brother was getting dismissed from the hospital. He had entered the hospital with high blood pressure and while he was there they pulled plenty of fluids off of his body. The day that he was getting ready to come home after being there three days, he was sitting on the side of his bed waiting to be discharged. I know how long it takes to get discharged from the hospital so I told my brother I'd run to the house and take care of a few little things and be back to pick him up at St. Francis. Before I could get out of the parking lot, my brother called me and told me I needed to come back. When I got back It was devastated. I found my brother in a state that was so heartbreaking. He was fine when I left him. He had suffered a stroke at the hospital. So he was moved off of the third floor up to the sixth floor, the neurology floor. I'll never forget the sixth floor. I stayed at the hospital night and day with my older brother. This is the brother that made sure his sisters and brothers were well taken care of when we were growing up. He had stepped to the plate to be the dad to all the sisters and brothers and I could not leave him like that, so night and day I stayed at the hospital. If my brother would breathe I would jump up off of the sofa. If the sheet moved I got up to see about him and I just stayed there in that room and prayed night and day. And I remember telling God that if he never, ever blessed me or gave me another miracle, if you never do anything else for me, I'm asking you to just stop by the sixth floor in this room and heal my brother. My brother deserves to live. And I would pray out and cry out to God night and day to just give R.L. his life and not suffer from that stroke. And I mean, God worked it out. R.L. went to rehab and little to say he didn't like rehab. He'd worked all his life, a very ambitious man, a man that's so aggressive he drives very hard and he's been a worker all his life. So he didn't know what it was like to be in a devastating situation like that.

As soon as R.L. got out of rehab he went home. He was home maybe about three weeks when, about four o'clock in the morning he got up to go to the bathroom and fell and broke his hip. That was a major setback. They had to go in and do surgery. Consequently, he had to start over in rehab. So we have dealt with a stroke, a setback of a broken hip and diabetes.

A month later my brother couldn't urinate properly, so one day when I had to go to Oklahoma City, my husband Eddie called and told me was taking R.L. to the hospital. When I got back from Oklahoma City I went to the hospital and found out the next morning that my brother was going on dialysis. So my brother has been on dialysis and it's been a traumatic experience for me to have to see my brother go through so much pain, but I always remained positive because I know that God is in the midst of my brother's healing and his miracle because of what I asked Him. I told God, my brother walked in this hospital, I want him to walk out. And R.L. did just that, through ups and downs, trials and tribulations. So every day, three days a week my brother goes for Pertonel dialysis.

My husband and I have been going to classes with him, learning all about it because, like you say, we are the caregivers. I am the caregiver for my brother and I recall one time a state worker came to my house. She was trying to explain to me about how I could be a family member and get paid for taking care of my brother. And I felt that was just robbing someone else of money that was needed to see about somebody else who is sick. My brother's in this household with me and I told the lady, I can't take any money from the state, this is my brother. I cannot be paid to take care of my brother when all he's done for me, taking care of me as a little girl, so all I'm doing is giving back, and I refused to accept any state pay at that time. And I still don't as of today. I use whatever money the Lord provides for us in this household and I take care of my brother the best I can, and I trust God for all things that I know that we can do this.

CHAPTER 20

After my brother suffered all his sickness, my husband retired military soldier, twenty-one years and nine months, retired veteran. He's not in the best of health. He got sick and he ended up in the hospital with pneumonia and congestive heart failure and he was told that he had a cyst on his kidney. I'm sitting here thinking, now God, I know you can't put any more on me than I can bear, and I know you won't. But through it all I have remained a very positive and strong person. Every day I pray and I ask God for strength. I know the race is not given to the swift, but to the one who can endure to the end. And I believe that. And I continue to pray for strength in this house, because I know that God can do all things and I know that God is a miracle, He always blesses those that are obedient and faithful to Him. So I continued to pray for my older brother, Ray Brannon III and my husband. I'm actually the caregiver for both of these men and I have a joy in seeing about them, waiting on them and we have a good time around this house. I thank God that He blessed me with this home. When my husband Eddie and I bought this home he had a bankruptcy sitting behind him, I had just gotten out of prison and we couldn't even see how we were buying this house. But I kept on pushing and believing in God for it. So this house that I have, I didn't understand why I had such a big house. But since I've been in this home, we have always had somebody here, a family member, somebody's been here. So I thank God for this house, and when people say, 'In my house I will serve the Lord' well, I say, 'In God's house' because this house is truly the Lord's because He gave this to Eddie and me. I had no credit, barely had a decent job, and like I said, Eddie had terrible credit. So we knew that God blessed us to have this home, and we give our glory to God, we open our home to anyone that has a righteous heart to do what's right by the Lord. So our house has been like a hotel, we always have someone here with us and we thank God for that because we share our home with love. As I stated before, God has blessed me to be a blessing to my family and I thank God for my wonderful husband.

I remember sitting in a courtroom back in January of 2004 as I was on the witness stand testifying, my husband had to listen to me talk about the man, how he raped me and tortured me and I recall one day after court we came home and my husband told me that the man who raped me was in the bathroom with him the same time he was. To hear my husband say what he said, I just couldn't believe it but I found it very supportive because he never says much of anything and he really doesn't show a whole lot of emotions, so when he made the statement that 'I started to piss on that man when I was in the bathroom', I thought, oh my God! This case had really disturbed my husband more than I realized. This case has been my life because I have strived so hard for justice on it that no woman should be abused and raped and tortured and there's no answers. Some women can't do anything about it but I think God gave me the ability, the knowledge, the staying power, the strength and the courage and grace enough to trust God that I can fight back. So my fight has been for so many women and children that can't speak out, can't stand up and fight, that I've been the force to show them that you can fight your attacker, especially if you know who they are. Don't let them intimidate you, don't let them silence you, don't be afraid. Trust God and He'll give you the strength and ability and He'll take fear away from you and put faith there. So that's what my fight has been about as well as thanking God for my wonderful husband standing by my side, in and out of the courtrooms with me, up and down the highway with me. I recall when I came out of trial in January of 2004, I was just like a little girl, devastated, I couldn't believe that so much evidence and so much truth, how does a man walk out of a courtroom with a not guilty verdict? I just couldn't understand it. And I was so devastated I was following my husband around the house like a little girl because I was just lost, I was confused. I really think at that point I had had a mild little nervous breakdown because I just sat up by Eddie and asked him, 'Eddie why?' I was scared. I was frightened at that point, I didn't know what to think because I couldn't believe a system could fail a person like that. I didn't understand that the trial was stacked. It was a sham. It was nothing but a joke to the judiciary system to allow a man to rape a lady with a glass salt shaker, lock little girls in a room and ask for sex and there were no charges put on this man. And then it reminded me that racists were very strong. Here's a black woman suing a white man that used to be a police officer, drivers examiner, had all this clout, all this status and here's this black lady with a criminal record, who could believe her? So that was the strongest objection I had to overcome, to stand against my past record. But God reminded me that everybody's got a past and nobody on this earth that lives does not have a past. But my criminal past was what the state officials used to steal a verdict from a woman that was raped. I understand today why women do not go into the courtroom. It is devastating. You're not only raped by the rapist, but the court system would rape you too. But you know what? God has been so good to me, it has not broken me down, I know what happened to me and I think we're fighting the state, I'm so strong in my conviction and I don't let shame and degrading stop me from speaking out. There's been times that I've been scandalized, been talked about, 'Girl, you're crazy to do this', 'What would you do to fight those people? They're going to hurt you.' Well I don't live in fear, I don't walk in fear, I know who my God is. And I remember every door that I have tried to go through, they've slammed in my face, but I continually remember that this job was called to me by the Lord and if you know the purpose that you're supposed to be walking in, you don't let anybody stop you. You just keep going because you know that God is guarding your footsteps. So I continue to fight the battle for justice. I promised God that I would speak in churches, that I'd go around the world, whatever He called me to do I would do it, because I feel like this is my calling. That I'm so passionate with it. I cry, I pray to God for helping the women who have been abused and so I know that this is my calling from the Lord, to stand up and fight and speak out of the goodness of God. I know that God brought me to this point and I'm so driven with it that I can't stop. And as many doors as I stated have been closed, but when those door close I laugh, because I feel like, if that door slams, there's a reason for that door to slam. Some doors that the devil thinks he closed would be some doors that God closed that He doesn't want you to walk through. Every door that opens may not be the one you need to walk through, so you have to seek God and trust Him to know that the doors that open and close, are they from the Lord? And many doors that have closed that I thought in my life were closed by the devil, God slammed some of those doors because some of that work was orchestrated by the devil for me to walk in and follow me to some of their traps. So I look back over my life and I thank God because I look at where I'm at today and look back at every door that was shut. They were shut, some of them, by the devil, but God also orchestrated some of those doors to shut because He knew that He had a purpose for me to see the doors shut because when the door's shut, He always opened a window for me to receive my blessings.

June of 2006 the with NAACP, we marched for justice for Darren in Stillwater, Oklahoma where Darren was murdered. The city police chief has done everything he could to assure us that they were looking for justice themselves. So we continued to march, continued to call on the FBI in Washington to look into this case. The national NAACP has taken on Darren's case to help us to arrive at some type of justice for Darren.

July 6, 2006. I went to Oklahoma City, hired an attorney named Joe Gloss. I gave him three thousand dollars retainer to file a writ to the United States Supreme Court on my rape case against the DPS and the State Drivers

Examiner. He, which I did not have knowledge, had previously been in prison, had some allegations against him for sexually asking clients for sex to work out some kind of agreement to represent them, some kind of tax evasions and I gave this man three thousand dollars and he told me he could get me to the Supreme Court in Washington. That never happened. I've been battling with him as far as trying to get my money back. I never visited this man, never one time by myself. I guess Roosevelt Milton knew that this man was not credible for some reason, and he always made sure that I went to go visit Mr. Gloss with somebody present with me as well as my husband or the NAACP.

Right now my case is at the Oklahoma Bar Association trying to use the Ethics Committee of the Bar Association to disqualify this man from the Bar. There's been numerous complaints on him. However, we were supposed to have this hearing on March 7th, it got postponed to a later date by the other attorneys on the other side, I'm sure. But I'm looking forward to going in and speaking on my behalf to try to get my money back as well as do whatever I can because these types of attorneys do not need to be able to practice and prey on the community like they do, lying, telling them they can take them to the Supreme Court when he can't even practice at the Supreme Court or in Federal Court, but he has a license to continue to be an attorney.

September 18 is my grandson's, my only grandchild's, birthday. I celebrated his birthday with him, did things with him, a precious grandson, a very smart grandson, very polite. His parents, which is my son Maurice and my daughter-in-law Lisa, have done a fine job. I pray that God continues to bless my grandson and keep His hands and my prayers on him and let him continue to grow up successfully and be the sweet young man that he is.

In October I celebrated my son's birthday, Maurice Smith. Maurice was my pride and Kyante is my joy. So I thank God for my pride and joy in my son and grandson. I didn't do much, just celebrated his birthday with my son

Maurice, my only son, who has been my best friend. He's been there for me when I was locked up, made sure I had money on my books and came to visit me. I know it was painful, because when you do time your family does time right along with you. When they send you money orders, that's doing time. When they come visit you in a place of confinement, it's painful and it's very hard. So after going through that I promised my son that I would never return to prison again unless someone messed with my children or my family. Other than that I have a good life. I have a foundation in the Lord, I know who I am, I'm comfortable in my skin. I look back over my life, reflect over so much pain that I have endured, upon my family as well as myself. The rape case has been very devastating to my family. I recall my son would bring Kyante up to visit me at DPS and just to hug and hold and see my son and grandbaby was a joy. Kyante was small and didn't understand what was going on. But neither did my son. He had no clue that I was paying the price of being raped to visit them, to allow them to come up and see me. I had to give this man sex in order to see my family and it was painful to do it, but to just hold your son and grandson and see that they're okay when you're confined behind prison walls. I think it was a dear price to pay but I did it out of love for my family because I do love my family. Without family you have nothing. The foundation of a family is unity, strength and forever family.

I have a little brother named Kermit Brannon. He's the baby of the bunch and he's terribly spoiled. He knows the Lord but for some reason my baby brother got on drugs and it seemed to have disrupted his life. But I opened my home for my brother to come spend with me as I've had several members of my family come, and I believe in God for a miracle in my baby brother. I always remind myself and tell Kermit, using myself as an example. I used to be on drugs, I've been in prison, I took a dive for the bottom, but God brought me all the way back up and I'm still not where I would love to be in my life, but I'm thankful to God for what He has made me today, and I strive everyday to reach a higher goal in my life for the Lord. My purpose is for God, not for anything else. It's to live and be a better person than I used to be. And I tell my brother Kermit all the time that, look at me, what God has done for me. I've been there, done that, and if He can change my life, He can change anybody because I thought I walked on air. I thought I was above the law and I was arrogant, caught up in Pamela, and I shared with my baby brother that prison wasn't a bad thing for me. It let me sit down and reevaluate my life, soul searching myself and looking at all my faults. So I tell Kermit all the time that he should submit himself to the Lord, not just give some of himself to the Lord, you have to give one-hundred percent, all of you to the Lord. In order for God to change us and make us, create a new spirit in us, we have to give our all to God. You can't give half of it to Him, you can't still drink and party and give Him sixty percent and you keep the other forty out there in the world, because God would rather have all of you than none at all, because you can't serve God and the devil too, you must submit your all and all to God. And I would tell Kermit, God has a purpose for you in life. Look at you and me, all the babies, we struggled without a dad. We struggled on everything that our brother R.L. taught us along with our mom. Our mother drank a lot. She was gone and my older brother would see about us, so we were the babies of the eight. We kind of grew up with what R.L. taught us, and what he didn't teach us we had to find out for ourselves. But I tell Kermit that if you get rid of the junk in your life, God will be able to replace you with jewels and all the silver and gold, but He can't get into your heart if you have hell in you. And my little brother knows that I love the Lord and I try to instill everything I can that's good in all of my family, because I don't want anybody to ever go down the path that I went down as far as going to prison. I did six calendar years in prison for checks and credit cards and that was a tough time, because while I was in prison, I lost two sisters and a dad, and you don't get to grieve when you're in prison with strangers as you do with your family. And you may not even get to attend a funeral or go to the hospital.

You have choices. "Terrible choices." The hospital or the funeral. And so I just knew that I tried to instill what I could that God has put in my heart for my baby brother because I desire for him to live for the Lord, and I know Kermit loves the Lord. And I tell him all the time to just submit it all to God, give it to the Lord and He will help you. And sometimes I do tough love on my brother. I'll never forget when I was in prison my older brother R.L. would send me money. And my big brother told me one time, he sent me a card and it just broke my heart, but I had to get out of prison and understand what he was saying. He said, 'Sister, this will be the last time that I send you a box of clothing, a TV or anything else to this address.' And he said, 'I'm not going to send you anymore money.' He sent me two hundred dollars. And I thought that was just so cruel of my older brother, knowing that I was confined and needed his help. But when I got out of prison I looked back over that, I revisited that card in my mind and I thank God today for that, because what my brother was telling me was that, as long as you return to prison or are in prison, you can have all these nice things sent in here, but he didn't want me to get comfortable in prison, he wanted me out of there. So at first I was mad at him and thought that was cruel of him to write me and say something like that when you're in a devastating place like prison, but I thank God for those words. I apply those words to my life everyday because those words that he said, I'm not going to send you anymore money or TV, boxes of tennis shoes, clothes, whatever to this address, and he was speaking of that prison address and I thank him for that because it let me know that he's not going to be there for me if I don't get it together. And he also said something to me that I said to my baby brother Kermit the other day which was, 'My brother told me a sermon is better seen sometimes than heard.' And I thought, how in the world do you see a sermon? I thought that you have to hear it. He was telling me that you have to walk that walk and stop doing that talking. And so I said that to Kermit. I said, 'Now you figure that out. I know a sermon is something that's preached, but walk this sermon instead of talking it and then people will believe you.' So I just thank God that He has been a blessing to me and to my family. But my baby brother's doing well. I told him, 'Look at me, I've been sober and clean for over twelve years. August the 10th of 2008 will be twelve years for me, sober and clean, I have no desire to return.' Rehab didn't do it. The Lord did it. I trust God. I had a made-up mind that I was not going to return to that type of life. I'd had enough. I was sick and tired. Rehab is good, but you must have a made-up mind. The Twelve Steps. The first step is God and if you follow that first step, the other eleven you don't need because He will supply you all of your needs. He will see you through it. You've got to pray and trust and lean upon God, lean upon the Lord for understanding. Not your understanding, but trusting of all things, that He will bring it to pass. Today I have no desire to ever do drugs again. It was like I asked God, if I ever have a desire to do drugs, make me so sick that I would think I'm dying, and you know what? One time I smelled the smell of some crack and it just made me so sick, and I remember asking God then. So you have to be careful what you ask the Lord because He sure will give it to you. He would grant it to you because he is the all-time God, and He's a God that cannot lie and His word does not come back void.

CHAPTER 21

September 6, 2006. I prepared my Writ to get to the Supreme Court. A letter was written to the United States Supreme Court asking them for more time to grant me on my Writ because the attorney in Oklahoma City had commissioned my funds and used thirty days of my precious time, so I wrote the Supreme Court a letter asking them to grant me more time. Justice Breyer wrote back granting me sixty more days. How grateful I was for that because I just didn't think they would do that.

November of 2006 my Writ was prepared and we got it out and sent it to the United States Supreme Court. This was the first time I had ever done a Writ and it was hard to do it pro-se. I sent forty books to the United States Supreme Court. The Supreme Court sent the box back to me, it was not prepared right. So I had to start all over. I recall going to Print Stop and I remember the name LeAnn, she would work, helping me to prepare this Writ, cutting it down, trying to make sure it was the right size, the right front and everything. So she helped me get the book ready, we worked on cutting that book for about two weeks. We got it ready to go to Washington to the Supreme Court. I had met this lady to type it up for me and get it all ready and once we got the book ready to go to the Supreme Court, we sent it up and it came back again. It still wasn't right. So after the book came back down from the Supreme Court, I had to start all over, all over. So by this time I had called and inquired about somebody that could help me type up the book and get the right measurements and do it right, because I had spent hundreds of dollars on this first set of books that was incorrect. So I had to find somebody, I found someone, the Lord blessed me with a lady named Irene Chance. She's the owner of Flying Fingers Typing Service. We called her up,

James and I, and we talked to her husband, Larry, and they told us he had to see the work. He wasn't guaranteeing they could do it because talking to someone on the telephone, you're not sure that they could do it. So we were just happy, believing in God, that we could get this done. We hung up the phone, happy and excited. James came up to Tulsa the next day or so and we met in Sand Springs at Flying Fingers Typing, met Irene and her husband, very nice couple, and so we laid out all the paperwork that we needed to get this book right this second time. She showed us that she could type it up and get it right. Well I guess in ten days she had it ready, so we got it ready, looked it over and everything was right and Larry recommended a company that could cut it down for us to get the book in the right measurements, everything right the second time. So we went to a little printing company and the gentleman assured us he could do it, which he did. We got the books ready, they looked wonderful. I prepared forty books for the United States Supreme Court again, three books for the Attorney General's office with proof of service included, and I got all of them in the mail and sent off. Well, at that time, I was just praying and believing in God that my Writ was going to be heard, and we got it off in enough time for the Supreme Court Justice to be able to read it. Once we got this done we just began to pray and believe God. I can recall calling James saying, James, you think it's going to be okay? And he would say, Pamela, just give it to God. We've done all we can do sister, just give it to God. So I tried to stay strong on that note, when the Writ was actually filed January the 4th of 2007, which gave the State until February the 5th to have their Answer to the Writ prepared.

On December 11th the State NAACP President Roosevelt Milton and James Carpenter along with someone else, met with the Attorney General's office. The Attorney General Assistant and Sharon were present in the meeting. They went on to tell him about the case. I was not present but I was informed of how the meeting went, that the Attorney General implied that he would put perjury charges on me. James told me that and I thought, wow, how could a man be so insensitive, but I realized that this is a blood-thirsty man that doesn't care anything about black people, because if he cared anything about people in general, all people, he would not be so quick to want to put perjury charges on a woman that's been raped so viciously by one of his state employees, but would use taxpayers' dollars to defend a man without realizing that this man resigned his job before the lawsuit was ever filed, which should have made him hire a personal attorney instead of the Attorney General's office using taxpayers' dollars to support him. So after that meeting was over, Roosevelt and James and I decided, well, we'll just show the Attorney General about perjury. We'll just come back with another press release. So that's when we came back on January the 4th with the press release to show him what we thought about his perjury charges and let him know that he's not intimidating anybody. He didn't intimidate James or Roosevelt and he certainly didn't intimidate me.

All that time, from January, we just waited patiently in the Lord. In January we started doing press conferences and got things ready for the public to know what was going on with the Writ at this point. So January the 4th, after we got it filed, we did a press conference in Oklahoma City. The State NAACP President, Roosevelt Milton, along with his legal team had me fax out press releases to all the newspapers. We did that. We went to Oklahoma City and did that press conference and for the first time I was so impressed that after all these years of begging the press to come forward, that so easily we may tell this story now because it was a State official that raped me and it was also the Attorney General's office involved in this major cover up on this case. So when I arrived in Oklahoma City to start getting everything prepared before the press release started, I was just amazed at how the press was coming in, because it was a case that made it to the United States Supreme Court. I was impressed with all the women that came out to support me. Women from DHS, the NAACP, the room was filled with women. I've never seen anything like that, which made me feel so good, because all these years I've been fighting and I felt like I'd been really heard. I knew that it was there but I never called upon many groups of women. Roosevelt's wife, Pat, got on the phone the night before the press release and she called everybody she could call to help in the show of support of this NAACP press conference as well as Pamela Smith, the rape victim. The press conference went great. For the first time in seven or eight years we'd never seen press like that.

After the press release was over, women were hugging me and wanting my story and just different people, men as well. We all got together and had something to eat at a little restaurant in Oklahoma City. We talked about it and went over the details of the press release. My friend, my brother, James Carpenter, and a lot of supporters, as well as my husband were there. We just had a good time.

CHAPTER 22

On February 2nd the State filed their Answer to the United States Supreme Court. However, they did not prepare a Writ. They evaded their responsibilities in answering that Writ. What they did was file a Waiver to the United States Supreme Court, waiving their right to even answer a Writ. When I heard that, I called the Supreme Court, just making sure the timeframe was all in on the State and the clerk told me, 'Young lady, they filed a Waiver, they didn't answer, they just said that they weren't going to answer and they filed a waiver' and I thought, well what an easy way out. How do you evade the Writ that I prepared because you can't respond to the truth when you even lied to the public and the jurors and everyone else on this case so viciously? I got mad for a moment because I wanted them to see how they were going to answer this Writ. How do you answer the truth when you lied for so many years? And at first it bothered me, so I said, 'Okay, thank you ma'am.' I hung up the phone and I thought about it and I laughed. Well, the deadline was February 5th, but they filed the Writ on the 2nd, I'm sure they did it electronically. On the 5th of February, time had passed and I didn't get a copy of the Waiver. February the 8th came along, of 2007. February the 8th came and I called the United States Supreme Court and they said that they had, confirming the Waiver had been filed. I said I had not received a copy of it, so I in turn hung up the phone and called the Oklahoma Attorney General's office. I got on the phone and said, 'Angela, this is Pamela. I have not received a copy of your Waiver that you filed.' She said, 'Oh, I put it in the mail.' I said 'I hadn't received it' like that old joke they say 'it's in the mail'. I didn't believe it because they had played so dirty on this case, haven't told the truth about anything, built this case on a sham and nothing but lies and a basic, major cover up. I said, 'Okay'. She in turn said, 'Can I have your fax number?' So I gave her my fax number. She immediately faxed me a copy of two pages, a front sheet and the Waiver by one of the Assistant Attorney Generals. So I immediately called up the Supreme Court and asked them if they could fax me one because I didn't feel like the Supreme Court, for some reason, had the same sheet that they had faxed to me. In turn, I got with a friend and I felt like they had maliciously, purposely, intentionally denied me my rights to be able to file anything to the courts. I was planning on filing the Amicus Brief, which is a friend to the court, which the NAACP was planning on doing, but the State utilized my time to be able to get the letters and everything prepared to get up there. So I in turn filed a Supplementary Brief back to the United States Supreme Court. Now that meant when the State of Oklahoma filed a Waiver, they waived all of their rights, they couldn't respond to anything else anymore. So once I got that filed, I sent forty more copies to the United States Supreme Court, then I sent three over to the Attorney General's office in Oklahoma City. I filed it on February the 16th of 2007 and got it to Oklahoma City. Now we're at the point when it was time for me to wait on the answer from the Supreme Court. The final answer. From February the 22nd, the last press conference, I found myself around the house very nervous, not understanding the court procedures at the United States Supreme Court and I didn't know what was going to take place. I would just pace the floor nervously.

March 1st, a Thursday, 2007. I called the Supreme Court just trying to get some information how the procedure goes. I got a lady on the phone and she told me that my case would go before the Justices on March 2, 2007 and that the Justices would vote on it. I hung up the phone saying thank you. On March the 2nd, I was nervous again. I called the Supreme Court and got this lady who said, 'This afternoon your case will be heard for the Justices to vote on it.' I said, 'Oh, would you pray for me?' And the lady said, 'Yes, I'll pray for you.' I was really nervous. I recall that day all I did was walk around the house crying, just crying, crying, crying. What I didn't know but had to come and realize that different people praise God in different ways. I humble myself in tears to the Lord. I'm anointed with tears from God I feel, because when I'm talking about God my eyes just water up with tears. So I recall all that Friday all I did was cry all day long. I'd praise God and just cry. I was in the back room and I recall just crying and my brother looked at me like, well sister, what's wrong? There wasn't anything wrong, I was just having that moment caught up with God and not knowing that God was preparing me, through my tears. Not only do I cry for happiness, I don't cry tears for sadness. My tears are tears of joy. And I realized when I was back in the back room crying, my brother thought something was wrong, but my brother and my husband know that I cry a lot, and they know when I'm crying it's always something to do with the Lord, praising Him or thanking Him. So it came to me that God was only preparing me for what He knew the answer was going to be on my case. And, because I worked hard, I worked for years to get to this point, fighting the enemy, how they lied, how they hid the glass salt shaker. Nobody to be trusted. People you thought you could go to for help you found you couldn't. So what I didn't know was the Lord was preparing me through those tears on Friday, and I found myself just down on my knees that Friday night, but what I realized in a couple of days or so was that God was preparing me for what the devil was going to try to use to take me out, make me depressed or even think about anything but praising God. I didn't know that at the time but that Saturday came, which was March the 3rd, I sat around the house reading my Writ over and over and over. I read the Writ so much I could tell you the story backward and forward and what everything was on one page. So I did that all day Saturday, looked at a little television, just real quiet, real quiet, then couldn't wait until Sunday morning came, which was March the 4th, 2007. I couldn't wait to go to church that Sunday morning. My husband got up and got ready to go to service with me. We went to my church called

Greater Love Temple, a wonderful church where I have a wonderful pastor, outstanding pastor's wife, loving church members. It's a small church but I go there to get my praise on, I feel so in touch with God in that church because no one is judged by anything but your love for each other and your love for the Lord. I remember being in church, just so happy and so peaceful. For the first time I realized I had some peace, that it was okay to let it go. You've done all you can do, Pamela, it's time to let it go, really let it go. And so I went to church that Sunday morning. After the church I was still in a good spirit, I barbecued that day, cooked my husband and my brother some steaks and some ribs and hot links and we just hung around the house and talked. I'm thanking God, always I thank God. I don't miss a moment of my day not praising God, giving Him some glory, some shout or something.

That Monday morning came, which was March the 5th of 2007. At nine o'clock that morning I got up to call the United States Supreme Court in Washington, DC, trying to find out what the answer was because I knew they voted on March the 2nd. I couldn't get anybody, I guess my time zone was different in Oklahoma than it was in Washington. I think it was nine o'clock here and ten o'clock there but I guess that people were just not at their desks, whatever. I didn't receive an answer. But Saturday night I had called James and said, 'James, I'm too nervous to hear the answer. I want you to be on the phone with me.' So he said, 'Okay' so I said, 'In the morning I'm going to get up and call them' which was that Monday morning. 'I'm going to call you and then I'll three-way and we'll hook up and talk to the people so we're here at the same time, 'cause I'm real nervous and I don't know if I could take the verdict.' He said, 'Okay.' When that Monday morning came I didn't hook James up on the phone. I said, 'You know what? I'm going to be brave by myself. I'm going to see whatever it is 'cause I see it, I know the Lord didn't bring me this far to leave me now. And I can stand and I can do this. So I'm going to hear it. I'm going to be a big girl and hear this.' So I called, like I said, didn't get an answer, so I guess about ten thirty I had called and I got this man. I had left the house, I got in my vehicle, went to the post office and after I left the post office I was driving back toward my home and I dialed the United States Supreme Court's office and I got this gentleman on the phone, who said his name was James. And I said, 'I'm calling to check on a case. Let me pull over because I don't know what the verdict is going to be.' I said this to the gentleman on the phone. 'I don't want to be, if it isn't in favor of me, I don't want to have a wreck or a nervous breakdown or something.' I thought, I don't want to be in traffic and get upset, so I pulled over. I said, 'My case number is 06...' I was so nervous I couldn't even rattle off my case number very well. I said, 'My case number is 06909.' I think I said 909. He said, 'Okay, the Petitioner's name?' I said, 'Pamela Smith. I am Pamela Smith.' He said, 'Okay. It was denied.' I said, 'Denied? You mean like I lost?' He said, 'Yeah.' At that point I said, how could they not help a woman that was raped? How could they turn down a case like this? Then he said, 'Well you know, you have twenty-five days to file for a Rehearing.' I said, 'Oh really?' He said, 'I've been here fifteen years and I've never seen that done.' I didn't say to him what I was thinking. I'm a child of God and I have favor with the Lord and I know what God can do. What you haven't seen in fifteen years, I'm gonna be the first, because I know what my God can do. This is what I was thinking to this man when he was saying it, but he was a very kind man. He was letting me know that I still had an option to come back and file for a Rehearing. So at that moment I knew that's what I was going to do, because I always felt that if you don't ever go to the end of your journey, you will never know what was there waiting on you. So I felt like, at that point I needed to go all the way. I have started from A and I was going past Z if I could. So I said, 'Okay, thank you.' I hung up the phone and I thought I was going to cry. Everything I thought I was going to do, no. Out of my mouth came 'thank you Jesus'. I didn't shed a tear. All the time I'd been crying and humbling myself, I hung up that phone, what I thought was going to destroy me turned out to be a blessing to me because what the devil did, he allowed me to submit myself to God through tears and prayer, put the full armor the Lord on me that weekend, that Friday, Saturday, Sunday, took a prayerful Monday, so whatever the verdict was, God had given me the strength to be able to stand and accept it and out of my mouth I recall saying, thank you God. Thank you Jesus. And drove off and came to my house and said, 'Now God, I need to continue to fight.' I remember calling James and saying, 'James, this is Pamela. The verdict didn't come down in my favor. But I'm okay. But this is what we need to do. We need to file for a Rehearing, a Petition for a Rehearing.' All James said was 'Okay. We'll do that.' So I found myself in a position to where it was really time for me to praise the Lord, because soon I would realize that there was that door that was shut, but I had to look back over everything I've done to know that it wasn't over. It's never over until God says it's over. And I realized at that point that the devil was only pushing me closer to my blessing, that's all he was doing. But on the same token God was strengthening me to be able to receive whatever it is that God wanted me to receive. Whatever it was it had to come from the Lord because that's where my trust and my faith lie.

On March 5th I told James, 'This is what we're going to do. We're going to fight even harder. Some of the information that we got we didn't put in that book. We're going to put it in there. We're going to hit them hard. We're going to give them everything.' So he started telling me things he wanted me to find, documents and everything, and I said, 'Okay.' I went through all my papers and got very serious documents that I had never pulled out before, got them ready to prepare to send back to Washington in a Rehearing. Well on March the 6th James had a lady from Oklahoma City come to Tulsa to meet with an attorney. He wanted me to meet with the lady and give her all my documents. I said, 'Absolutely not. So I recall my baby brother calling that he needed to go to Cushing because he was trying to get a job, that they had called him that morning for an interview. So I said, since I'm going to Cushing, which is in the same direction, I'd just go onto Oklahoma City and take them myself and put them in James' hands. We went to Cushing, Kermit got his job, he was so grateful, so happy, he was going to make twelve dollars an hour working at the oil company. I remember he and I just talking. I said, 'Kermit, when you align yourself up and are obedient to God, you position yourself for a blessing from God. God rewards His children who are good.' And that's the same way I did as a parent to my son and to my grandson, is that I believe that when your children do well, you reward them good, and that's how the Lord treats His children. He rewards us good, because when we do good deeds, we're rewarded for those things. And it's okay to look for rewards from God because we are heir to everything He owns so there's nothing wrong to look for those blessings from God. So I told Kermit that I had a home in my name in Cushing and I told my baby brother, 'This is my chance to help you. You've been down for so long. And as long as you're trying, I'll help you.' So I let him have a house that belonged to all of us but was in my name. I paid the taxes on it, did all the work to keep it up, to keep it cleaned and everything and I said to him, 'I'm going to give you a home. The Lord blessed me with a twenty-two hundred square foot home. I don't need two homes. I can't live in two houses at the same time and you don't have a home so I want to bless you to have a home. I'll put this deed in your name and you'll have your own place. There's nothing like having your own roof over your own head so you don't have to depend on living with anybody or somebody putting you out of their home. He was so grateful.

After that we went onto Oklahoma City to take the documents. This is still March 6, 2007. We were listening to church music going down the highway. We were just talking and rejoicing in the Lord. When we got to Oklahoma City we went to James' house, pulled up and got out. James opened the door and let us in and my baby brother went in the back room and James and I were in the middle of the room where he takes in all of his business for his clients, helping them. He's over the legal redress team. We went in and sat down and talked. I told him how I cried that Friday and how I prayed to God that whole weekend and how I couldn't wait to go to church and I said, 'James, it came to me today, I want to tell you what was dropped in my spirit to me. The Lord said, I did not bring you this far to leave you now.' I said, 'James, we're not going to quit. We're going to go all the way because you know what? So many people quit when they're just so close to their blessing. They throw their hands up. I don't let lawyers and court rules tell me no when I know God will say yes. When you know you know, you follow the Lord.' So I told James how we're going to do this. We're going to take this police report of Candace's, this evidence that came from the District Attorney's office, this information sheet that tells where the glass salt shaker was. Some information on the sheet I didn't understand, police words I guess. We're going to use this and we can have up to fourteen or fifteen pages and we can only have so many to go back in this Rehearing Petition. And I recall looking at James and thinking to myself when I was looking at him and talking with him, this is the man that the State has abused, stripped him because he blew the whistle in 1979 and told the DPS officials that there were officers of the State at the Attorney General's office having sex with inmates. So he came under scrutiny, he became a target because he spoke out against evil doers. I looked at him sitting there and I thought, Lord, you have got to bless this man. Even if it means bless me, let me bless him. And I looked at him and tears were in my eyes because he has a good heart to help people. I said, 'James, you know when I told you we were going to keep going? God had really showed me that you were going to do it because look at you, there's so much peace about us continuing this battle. We haven't quit. We don't want to quit. We know the truth in this case.' And that's what happens, so many of our people, or even people in general, quit. They give up because the courts beat them down. And people get tired and they say, 'Oh it won't do any good. I'm going to just quit.' I've been fighting for ten years. I have not stopped. I haven't come up for air in a long time because I know this journey that I'm on for justice is to help so many women around the world. While I was sitting in James' office we called the Supreme Court and I was trying to find out how the judges voted. Could they tell a number who voted for you? Kind of like get a survey, an analysis how many voted? The lady said it was four judges and it takes four of them to be unanimous.

CHAPTER 23

On March 5, 2007 I called to find out the decision. It was made, my case was denied before the United States Supreme Court. I was very hurt and disappointed but I knew it was not the end of the journey for me, that I still had more options. If there's options on the table take them because rape is something that's very devastating and it changes a person's life forever. Your life will never be the same. You know that your faith and your hope and your confidence and trust lies in the Lord, but deep down inside you know that your life has been forever changed. You are not whole, the Silent Coalition made sure of that, I'm damaged but still strong. Rape changes you forever, but it doesn't control my life. I choose to be a fighter against rape. Don't let rape defeat you.

On March 6, 2007 I called the Supreme Court clerk's office and I believe I talked to a clerk. I wanted to know how the judges voted. What's the standard of how they conduct their decisions? And the clerk told me that it takes four to vote for the writ to be passed through. She also indicated to me that this case is put on the Internet and it is read all over the world and also that different presses could pick it up and that it's a case that everyone would have their eyes on.

I called the Supreme Court in the presence of James Carpenter. James is the person who diligently has helped me to put this Writ, my Supreme Court Supplemental Brief and the Petition for Filing for a Rehearing together. God has certainly used this man. James was robbed of a million dollar judgment as well by the State of Oklahoma. He has been abused and mistreated through the system. He is the one that had exposed, back in 1979, that the inmates at the DPS had been abused and mistreated. So by him speaking out, being the whistle blower or whatever you want to call him, I call it being a man standing up to the plate and doing the right thing.

Kermit and I left James' house, stopped at a restaurant to eat, stopped by my Aunt Mae's in Oklahoma City and she gave me three bras. I have such a heavy chest and my auntie, my only aunt that I have living, gave me some bras and we visited for awhile, then left, stopped to get gas and headed on home back to Tulsa.

When Kermit and I had reached the outskirts of Tulsa, there was a young black lady broken down on the highway. I was going about sixty-five or seventy miles an hour and I looked to my right and saw her walking toward her car which was broken down, so I had gone probably about a half mile down the road and pulled over and backed up all the way to go back and help the young lady. I recall telling Kermit that that could have been me, as many times as I had traveled down the highway, but God protected me and saw about me to where I never broke down. So I thank God because I stopped to help that lady because I just felt like it was the right thing to do and I felt compelled to help her. Kermit helped fix her car. Her pedal was sticking so Kermit tied it together so she could get home. A very nice Christian lady, told me she was a single mom just trying to raise her son, her only child. So anyway, Kermit and I proceeded to Tulsa, I dropped Kermit off at home and headed onto my house.

Thursday, March 8, 2007. I called the Stillwater Chief of Police, about a meeting that Roosevelt Milton had planned with the FBI to meet on behalf of my nephew Darren who was murdered in Stillwater. I invited the Chief to the table to sit down with us to discuss this case intelligently so the Chief of Police can make sure that me, the NAACP and the FBI all are on the same accord, looking for the right answers to achieve justice for my nephew Darren. I also let him know that the meeting was going to be held on March 13 at nine a.m. at the Jimmy Stewart Building in Oklahoma City, the NAACP's headquarters where they meet in Oklahoma City.

March 8, 2007. I have an older brother who is on dialysis and I'm a caregiver to him, and my brother takes a class from one o'clock until about three o'clock or three thirty. My husband and R.L. went to his training class. He's going for hemodialysis, so we did the training class together. Then I received a call from James letting me know that to file my Writ for Rehearing we needed to start preparations, get it to the typist then get it cut down, copied and sent as this would be our last chance of having my case go before the United States Supreme Court.

I left that Thursday after my brother finished his class. We got on the highway heading to Oklahoma City. My brother's a crippled guy, but he didn't want his little sister on the highway by herself so even after doing a class of several hours, he wanted to ride with me. My husband could not go because he had plans the following Saturday to drive his son-in-law to the clinic in San Antonio to have laser surgery on his eyes. So my older brother and I rode down the highway together, had a good time. We played music, we talked, we visited, we played Gospel music then we played a little Temptations' music. On our way there, and once I arrived at James Carpenter's home in Oklahoma City to pick up the filing for the Rehearing, James and I went over the Writ together, and in one part of that Writ it read that James was challenging Clarence Thomas, the black justice of the United States Supreme Court. We didn't know how they voted because we were informed earlier that it takes four, but James was under the assumption that Clarence Thomas must have not voted for us, so in the Writ James had challenged Clarence Thomas to remind him that he went through a situation similar to mine, although he was the accuser. So in that, it was very heart wrenching and I laughed when James was reading it to me, letting Clarence Thomas know that he doesn't have to be so hard on black people that just because him and his problems with Alicia Halter he doesn't have to be mad at the whole black race. On the way home I was telling my brother that I had told James I did not want to put that in that Writ because if we're going to get any justice from the Supreme Court, I don't need to tick them off. James said, "It's the truth, Pamela," and so God tells us to speak up to people, we need to say what's in our hearts and quit being afraid to say it. And I admire James for putting it on paper because to me I feel in my heart every black, not every black person but the majority of black people, feel that Clarence Thomas, the black United States Supreme Court Justice, is mad at his race of people because of the situation he went through with Ms. Halter, being accused of his sexual harassment in his situation. I laughed about it and I was telling my brother about it. My brother said, 'Sister, if you're ever in doubt you should always say no. That was my older brother R.L. speaking to me and I said, 'You know what? That's always been my philosophy, if ever in doubt always follow your first mind and say no and then you'll never go wrong. So I said when I get home I will read this to you brother and let you hear exactly what is said.' So I got him in the house, got him in the back room and sat him down, we went over the brief. He said, 'Now sister, don't say that because it may be the truth but don't say it because you're looking for help.' I remember somebody saying, oh Lord, you're putting that case before the Supreme Court, Clarence Thomas isn't going to give any justice. He isn't going give you relief. He's mad at all black people. So I don't know if that's true or not true but in my heart I kind of entertain there is bitterness still there. I'm not the one to say the man was guilty or not guilty. I can only speak of what happened to Pamela Smith in her case and that I was hoping for Justice in it. And for all I know he could have voted for me. I don't know which way the Judges voted at the Supreme Court. But anyway I just found it very amusing. We don't expect Clarence Thomas to vote for a rape case because I'm a black woman but we do expect him to look at the law, follow the evidence and listen to the testimonies, look at the corruption that is in the case and follow the law. My Constitutional rights were violated and we could not get the district court, lower courts, the Tenth Circuit Courts of Appeal, nor the United States Supreme Court to justify my rights. These are the same people that helped the prisoners in Abu Grey who were abused and showing their bodies. The United States took care of those foreigners but you mean to tell me that the United States cannot listen to my cry? The United States Supreme Court Justices cannot listen to the cry of their own? I am a citizen. I am an American citizen. I was raped, tortured, forced by instrumentation of a glass salt shaker and the state officials violated every rule of law, every state law, their oath of law. Everything that they possibly could do in this case because I was black, powerless and an ex-inmate, I had no voice and they let this man get away with rape. I know he's not the first one but I vow to myself, the Lord and other women that I will not give this journey up. I was going to see this through. So in saying all of that, we did not expect Mr. Thomas to be the one that we were looking to be the Savior. My God, my Lord, my Rose of Sharon, my Lily of the Valley, my Jehovah God, that's who I look to for answers. That's who I look to for help in a time of trouble. That's who I look to when I'm sick or need a healing. That's who I cry on, that's who I cry to for justice in my life. It has been nobody but the Lord that has seen me through this case. If I looked to man for help all these years I've been fighting for justice, I would not have made it this far. Man will turn their back on you. They will lie to you. They will deceive you. They give up. They don't stand in the storm. When the storm comes, they run for cover. When God tells you to stand, be still and know that He's Lord. You have to do that. You have to go through trials and tribulations in life. You just can't think that here comes a storm, I better run for cover. When God is before you, who can be against you? And when God calls you to do something you do it. When God called Moses, he told Moses to go. Moses asked God, 'Well, what will I say?' God told him to just go and open your mouth and I'll speak. And that's what I've been doing all these years is open my mouth and let the Lord speak for me because I know that this fight does not belong to me. I did not do this for Pamela. I was called to do this because the Lord called upon me to do it. Anytime a person has to go through this much pain, the suffering, and the state officials do everything they can to try to shut you down, to keep your story from being told. Every time they shut down this story, it has allowed another victim to become a victim of a rape case, rape abuse, sexual harassment. I know I can't stop rape but I can certainly put the word out and be a voice for many victims that are ashamed to come forward, ashamed to speak out. Yes, it is the worst and the most degrading thing I've ever done in my life. I've never ever encountered anything so devastating as this rape case. It has not been enough to make me quit because when you make a promise to God you don't quit. You continue to go on. You keep fighting and fighting even if the doors keep closing. Just remember, God must know what he's doing. He's a God that makes no mistakes, and you have to know that. And when you know you know you know, you know. Now, when my case went before the Supreme Court, the state had done everything they could to manipulate this case. But there is one thing I know, I have the truth on my side. I know I was raped. I know what the state officials did. They used seventeen witnesses to get on the witness stand back in January 2004 and lie. Make up things. I never stole cash money from an old lady in a wheelchair. That's a lie. I never danced on a table. I never did anything but tell the truth about this case. And it's sad when a rape victim can come forward. That's why so many victims do not come forward because of the garbage that comes with it, the trash, the scandalizing, the degrading. As I always said, it has not been enough to stop me because the more I talk about this case it helps me to heal and I certainly hope I've been a voice for everyone else, especially victims of rape. To continue to be a voice for these victims, to let them know that there is someone that is looking out for them. Looking out to be able to help victims that have been abused of such horrific crimes as rape.

March 9, 2007. I got up at nine a.m. and called Larry, Flying Fingers, and told him I wanted to bring over the information to start getting my petition typed up and ready for the rehearing. Larry told me to come on over so I left

Tulsa and drove over to Sand Springs, Oklahoma, to a company called Flying Fingers and met with Irene and Larry. Irene and I went over the information to get it prepared and I read to her about the part about Clarence Thomas that James had put in the Writ. I had scratched it out but I could still read the information on the paper because I just scratched through it that I didn't want that said. So I read it to Irene. First of all I asked Irene if she knew of Clarence Thomas and she said yes. So I read to her what James had put in the Writ and we laughed so hard. We laughed about it because we knew that there was probably not going to be any justice from that situation but we laughed and thought it was funny. And we moved on so we went through the information getting the Writ ready and I told her I needed it to be ready by at least by next Tuesday or Wednesday.

However, she had been working on my book for me. I started this book because it was time to write it. This story needs to be told. I have had people for ten years telling me, Pamela, you've got a story that can help so many women. The fight, the journey, the strength, the things that you've gone through in your life and that how God has brought you through it. So many things that you've gone through in your life that, and you're still standing. I choose to write this book simply because I knew it was the story to tell, especially about rape because it's the most vicious thing that can happen to a woman or a child or anyone. Rape has no color and when a person's going to rape you, they don't look at what color you are. They just know they're going to victimize you, take something that's not theirs, violate you, change your life forever. Your life is forever changed no matter what. Nothing in the world can ever repair the damages that the State of Oklahoma has done to me. The State Driver Examiner, the man that raped me, tortured me, violated me, this man knows he raped me. This man has never come to a television camera and denied it. He will never speak to the press. They say, well why would he have to if he didn't do it? Well, I think that if a person did not do any of the things that he was alleged doing, I would come out swinging. I would swing with everything I've got, because first of all a woman that was not raped I don't think would be chasing this much pain around the world and seeking this much justice and spending all the money that she has fighting the case. So therefore, this man has never stepped up to the plate to be a man to say this lady's lying. And I just hope and pray someday that this man in his heart will find the peace he needs and surrender his life to the Lord and stop practicing being a Christian and be a Christian. During the trial he testified that he was practicing being a Christian. Now I have a problem with that. I don't know how you practice being a Christian. Either you are a Christian or you're not. You don't practice. I understand you becoming into the babyhood, when you're a baby you learn how to walk step by step but there's no such thing as practicing and being a Christian. You either live by the Lord or you don't. The word practicing, I don't understand. This is not a basketball game. This is not a football game. This is not a dance recital. This is not a hip hop show. You don't practice for the Lord. You either do it or you don't. So I don't understand the term 'he was practicing to become a Christian.' I felt that very offensive because every time I ever came to the Lord, I wasn't practicing. I don't know where in the Bible that it ever said that if you practice you can become a Christian. I may have fallen short to the Glory of God but that doesn't mean, okay, I didn't do it right, I'm going to practice and then do right. And to allow the Attorney Generals to say such thing as becoming a practicing Christian.

After James Carpenter, a former OHP Trooper, a Christian man, a man of faith, and I had a discussion at his house about this information that he had put in there about Clarence Thomas and we talked about it, we laughed about it and he said, 'Yeah, put it in, put it in.' I said, 'Well, James, I don't know if I need to say that because I'm the one that's looking for help from the Supreme Court and I would not want him coming back trying to sue me for anything.' The American dream is suing people. That's the American way.

So I didn't want to put it in there. I told James, 'Let me read it and let me pray about it. Let me see if this is something God would want me to say.' So he said, 'Okay, okay but it's the truth, it's the truth.' Later on that Thursday night, I believe it was March 8, 2007, after I got home I received a phone call about ten p.m. After answering, James was on the other end and he said, 'Pamela, you do what you want to do. If you want to take that out of there, I don't have a problem with that because I want you to feel comfortable.' I said, 'Well, I'm going to read it.' I had not read it really to dissect it and meditate over it. I said, 'Okay, James, you know we don't want to alienate anyone. We're not trying to tick anyone off, although it may be the truth, but right now we're looking for justice and looking for help. We're looking for true justice through my rape case' and so he said if I found anything else in that Writ that I wanted to add or take out, feel free to do it because it has been the Lord, James and myself that have sat down with the wording and the knowledge to put this Writ together. So we not only wanted to feel like we were better than the Supreme Court, we didn't want to send any messages that we were disappointed or bitter or angry with the U.S. Supreme Court for not ruling to hear this case, but we also wanted to let it be known that we were looking for them to do the right thing because the lower courts had failed tremendously. We have a Governor in the State of Oklahoma who has a first cousin that is a Judge at the Tenth Circuit Court of Appeal, so even in my Writ it tells how the Governor of Oklahoma's cousin swore him in. We were showing a pattern that there is connection or tithe with the Governor and the Judge being first cousins and both of them from the State of Oklahoma, Shawnee, Oklahoma. So, therefore, we were trying to establish the pattern that this is why I myself was not getting justice on this case because there were roadblocks and that we had begged the Governor of Oklahoma through many letters, through tapes, attempted several times to have visits with the Governor, and he would turn a deaf ear on the case. So on the same token, we didn't want to come back and alienate another judge if they felt like we were targeting the judges. So James did tell me to take that out if I didn't feel comfortable with it. I did speak to my brother, I did pray about it and sometimes you don't always have to go to God about things. My pastor always said when it comes time to give, you ask them to give and they say I've got to pray about it. You don't have to bother God about every little gory detail. God expects us to have common sense about some things so we don't have to go disturb God all the time for little bitty things. God is a big God. He hears every one of our moans, our complaints, our praises, our thank you's, our disappointments, our failures, whatever, God hears it. So I felt like I did need to talk to God about this but then I didn't have to talk to God long because it was so clear that it was too harsh to say what he said in the letter. I do recall speaking to one of the clerks at the U.S. Supreme Court and the clerk was reading off all the cases that were getting ready to be heard or had been heard before the Supreme Court and I recall asking the clerk when she was reading, you mean to tell me there are no rape cases on there? She said no. If you listen to today's news, every news station out there, every one of these broadcasters got a case of some type of rape, abuse, sexual harassment and here is a top profile case where a lady was raped in a drivers license agency, an inmate, powerless, helpless, vulnerable, a ward to the state, and raped in a state building repeatedly, one time with a glass salt shaker. Young girls going into a driver's license agency, trying to obtain a driver's permit and the defendant soliciting these ladies for sex for their licenses, and the State of Oklahoma turned a deaf ear because it was to save the state money and embarrassment. Then when we lean upon the U. S. Supreme Court and the U.S. Supreme Court can help foreigners, their bodies have been exposed and their Constitutional rights are being violated and that's cruel and unusual punishment. To have a glass salt shaker shoved up a woman's vagina, how much cruel and unusual punishment does the Supreme Court need to be able to see and furthermore, how come they could not see the obstruction of justice there? I recall watching the Scooter

Libby trial. They put obstruction of justice on this man for lying to a Grand Jury. Well, what happened to the Lieutenant with the DPS that brought a glass salt shaker, that the victim, Pamela Smith, told where it was that the man shoved it up her vagina. He went and retrieved it, brought it to me to identify, but when the time came to go to trial, January 6, 2004, Civil trial and Grand Jury trial, there was no glass salt shaker. He left it in his desk. Also, he never did turn it over to the District Attorney's office for evidence and for possible criminal charges filed upon the defendant.

CHAPTER 24

Today is Tuesday, March 13. I'm getting ready to meet with the state NAACP, Mr. Roosevelt Milton, and the head agent of the FBI in Oklahoma City along with another family, whose son was murdered by an officer, allegedly murdered, and there will be topics we will discuss. We will talk about Darren Brannon that was shot down, killed in Stillwater and the FBI wants to meet with Roosevelt. I told Roosevelt I wanted to meet with the FBI as well, that this is my family. My nephew was murdered and his mother's dead and there is no one to speak for him. His father has never been there for him and I'm going to speak for my nephew and I will continue to stand for my loved ones that even if they were not dead, I would speak and be a voice for them. So we are meeting with them today to talk about Darren. I told my older brother the other day, 'R.L., you know what brother, I'm going to meet with the FBI, not to discuss my rape case. This is about Darren.' I don't want to waste my time talking to these people about me. I'm still breathing, I can fight. I need to be a voice for Darren and today I will talk about Darren. I believe that this man murdered my nephew in cold blood for no reason other than he was born black. I will stand in the gap for Darren Keith Brannon. My sister is deceased and I will be the voice for that young man. I will not stand by idling, just doing nothing. So today we meet with the FBI, nine o'clock a.m., at the NAACP headquarters in Oklahoma City.

I will meet my husband, Eddie, in Oklahoma City. He spent the night in Lawton and we talked last night and I told him to just spend the night there. You know, he's been going so much lately so I told him to just spend the night and meet me in Oklahoma City at the Jimmy Steward Building to meet with the FBI, so that's our plans for today.

Today is Tuesday, March 13, 2007. I met with the FBI today at nine a.m. Roosevelt Milton, the State President was present. Clarence Powers, the legal redress, former Oklahoma City Police Office, my husband Eddie, my brother Raymond Brannon, which we call R.L., and myself was present, along with the Chief of Police from Stillwater, Oklahoma, as well as Mr. Tittle who was the investigator on my nephew Darren Brannon's case in Stillwater. A good meeting. We all formally introduced ourselves to the FBI agent, Mr. Mike Brown, the new Special Agent in charge for the State of Oklahoma with the FBI. We discussed Darren's case, my rape case and I provided documents for Mr. Brown to keep. Roosevelt went over several cases with the FBI agent, Mr. Woods, letting him know about the status of different cases in the State of Oklahoma. I spoke up and told them about my nephew Darren, how I felt like that the District Attorney dropped the ball in the case to allow a man to hunt a man down with a rifle and blow his heart out and nothing be done about it. And besides, Darren was married to a white lady and they had two children and I felt like the landlord who had a contract with Janine instead of Darren Brannon, which they were common law husband and wife, that he killed Darren because he was born in the time that racism was very strong. I shared those thoughts with the FBI and the group that was present today. I felt very positive they were going to take that information and process it. I provided him with a lot of documents on my rape case as well some information about Candace Rowe, the little fifteen year old girl that the same man who raped me locked her in a room and asked her for sex. I provided several documents for this agent today. A very pleasant meeting. After the meeting my husband and I went to the hospital to visit my husband's sister, Virginia. She was in ICU doing about as well as can be expected. We had prayer. I left my husband at the hospital, I had to get home because I have a brother that's not well himself but through the Grace of God I know that he will be continually making a remarkable progress in his healing that God has put upon my older brother, R.L.

We arrived in Tulsa today, picked up my grandson Kyante from school, stopped by McDonalds, got him something to eat and headed home. I did speak with Irene today and she let me know that my Petition for Rehearing on the Writ was ready today and tomorrow, which is March 14, I will pick up my Petition for the Rehearing, get it prepared and off to the U.S. Supreme Court. This is my second attempt to go to the Supreme Court. I will exercise every right that I have in seeking justice. I do believe that this FBI agent it going to look closely into this case. I did tell him how the Lieutenant of OHP violated the rule of law, how he did not preserve the evidence, to put it in the property, so if there were criminal charges to be placed upon this man they were not. I spoke with the FBI agent about that so I'm just hoping that somewhere along the line that in this Petition for Rehearing I was very strong in my conviction to the U.S. Supreme Court. I let them know if you all do not hear the cry of Pamela Smith, please listen to the voice of so many women in prison that are being abused and I felt like they are sending a message to the jailers and all these de facto prison guards, state officials, police officers, troopers, whoever these people are that are in charge of inmates, and violating these women and taking advantage of these women because they're powerless, they're vulnerable, they're helpless, and so I felt that the Supreme Court of the United States has turned their back on powerless women and men that are locked up. Yes, they made a mistake. I made a mistake but it does not constitute rape. The State Statute in Oklahoma says that if you have sex with an inmate it is called rape. There is no such thing as consent. And during the trial I believe that the judge gave the wrong jury instructions or did not make himself clear to these people. These people thought it was a consensual sex relationship and I don't know what got into these people's mind but if the law was clearly laid out to them I do believe this verdict would have been different.

Today is March 14, 2007 at eight thirty a.m. The nurses from Saint Francis stopped by this morning to train Eddie, me and my brother on his Pertonel Dialysis. He's been doing chemo and today he will start on his home dialysis. The training was successful. Around eight thirty-five a.m. I returned a call to New York City to the Urban League to a lady by the name of Sally Heli who had called me yesterday to check on how my rape case was going and have Reverend Albert Harpon with his organization contact me. She had given me his address and information and I indicated to Ms. Heli that I had not heard from Reverend Harpon. She wanted to know what is it she could do to help and she gave me some organizations to contact. I also asked her if she could contact some national media, that this case needs to be exposed because if she helped me, it would be helping many other women around the world that are lockup and being abused. Rape victims as a whole, not just female offenders, anybody who's being raped and doesn't have a voice to speak out. She was so willing and so kind. I never met the lady in person, just had some documents with the Urban League's name on it and contacted them and she became attentive to my needs, concerned enough to want to help. So I asked her would she e-mail some organizations and do what she could. She said she would see what she could do to help and so that's what we did.

Around eleven thirty a.m. on March 14, 2007, I left my home to see Irene in Sand Springs to pick up my Petition for Rehearing, get it ready for the printer today and get it out of here and back to the U.S. Supreme Court. So I will be making preparations to get it out on March 15, 2007 to the U.S. Supreme Court and we'll forward three copies to the Oklahoma Attorney General's office as well as several copies to the news media and to James Carpenter, the State President and other family and friends. So at this point my Writ will be leaving tomorrow March 15, 2007, waiting on the rehearing from the Supreme Court.

In April of 2008, my Petition for Rehearing was denied again, I was once again faced with another court battle lost. I've been begging for justice since I started this journey, and I have always been given the Silent Coalition. I vow to never give up until I know it was from God and God has given me the chance to do the book. It is not always right in life, but it is always right to do the right thing and this book gives me all the vindication I need. No one can stop the truth from going forward and no one can tell the untold side the way I can. I was raped repeatedly and that will always be the truth.

On June 16, 2008, Senator Inhofe's office in Oklahoma City had a meeting with myself, James Carpenter and Roosevelt Milton, President of the NAACP Oklahoma City branch spoke of how they let down a case with over 20,000 documents, eleven years of crying in pain, three courtroom failures, and Senators, Representatives, Constituents gave us fifteen minutes. There is no justice for a woman when she takes a strong stand against violence and scary state officials. We were hoping that the Washington Senator would help get the D.O.J. involved and look at the cover up the in justice and the corrupt not only in this case but in the State of Oklahoma cover up. I had received several letters from a Washington Senator, no help, passing the case onto Oklahoma Senators Inhofe and Tom Colburn. On July 17, 2008, I received a letter from Senator Inhofe stating on my behalf that the United States Department was not favorable on my behalf and investigation into the rape case by the State Driver Examiner.

On July 18, 2008, I received a call from Senator Tom Colburn's office about a meeting I had requested back in August 5, 2007 when I went to Washington, DC, along with some member of the Oklahoma NAACP. He wanted to let me know why he didn't meet with us, after all the expense I went through to go, and shuffled appointments before we left Oklahoma. Our scheduled meeting with this Oklahoma Senator will now take place a year later August 4th, 2008, at the Senator's office. I went to a meeting that the Senator spoke at in June 2008 and I confronted him about why he was in the Tulsa Library today meeting with people and he couldn't meet with his constituents that travel to Washington. He apologized.

Begging for Justice, the Silent Coalition. I never will

get over all the injustice that the system failed me, but I believe that many have suffered and may not know it but how do you go through this life and it doesn't come around, maybe not to those professional liars and all the people that wronged me, and to Candace Rowe, and other victims. I'm a strong believer of what goes around comes around. If it goes up, it must come down. I hope that my story will help victims that have been abused. Fighting for justice has given me some relief because I faced the pain of rape and had to allow my pain to be turned into this book. I refused to let someone make me become them. Even when it is to forgive and heal, knowing you know the truth, never give up.

CHAPTER 25

Monday, August 4, 2008. I got a call from the former County Commissioner, Wilbert Collins, telling me about an ad in the *Talk World* about Senator Tom Colburn not meeting with his constituents on this day. I had a meeting with Senator Colburn and his staffer, Dan, Senator Maxine Horner, James Carpenter, Wanda and Clarence Powers. The meeting was another let's see, I have hopes that this Senator can help me. He told me that he would see if my civil rights were violated and he would fly in his attorneys from Washington to look at my case. How excited I was but I've been there before with a lot of promise. There was something about this Senator that I took him to be really serious about justice. I wanted to shake his hand because he was offering me something that no one else had. Someone to look into my civil rights. In the last eleven hours I'm still holding out faith that my begging for justice is not in vain. Now it is wait and see. I told him how I was offered sixty thousand dollars to settle this rape case, and how I declined the money and went to court and got beat up by the lady attorney for the State. But my faith has not wavered. I recall my Bishop, Donald Tyler, telling me, 'Pamela, everything that devil stole from you, God will make them give it all back." I recall when I took from someone the courts made me pay it all back, so my God has truly kept me in His presence. I believe that.

On September 3, 2008, at 2:00 pm, I met with Senator Colburn's staffer, Sarah Beth Groshart. She flew in from Washington to have the closed meeting with James Carpenter and myself to tell us that because of the Separation of Power that the Senator could not help us. Only from a Federal level. I thanked her and told her that this battle belongs to God and I'm getting out of the way.

No help came to me, my last time begging for justice.

In the coming year, 2009, I plan to revisit Washington, DC to be able to meet with Senators and Congressmen to stop prison rape and abuse and inmates' constitutional rights.

What Pamela Smith and Candace Rowe would like to see happen on this case:

1. Be vindicated.
2. Admit he (DPS Examiner) is guilty.
3. Criminal charges on DPS Examiner and all that violate the law.
4. Attorney General and staff along with OHP, District Attorney, and DOC publicly apologize for all the injustice they caused Pamela Smith, Candace Rowe and James Carpenter, OHP, our families and mislead both juries on each case.
5. Compensation for the damages left on Pamela Smith and Candace Rowe.
6. Put an opinion and overturn House Bill 2966 in the State of Oklahoma against inmates.
7. Feds to police in prosecuting more rape cases on inmates behind the prison walls and that DPS males are not alone with females during driving tests by having female driver examiners for women and girls.
8. Re-open the Rape Case, and the Soliciting Sex From a Minor, Request by the United States Justice Department and the Washington FBI to seek our Constitutional Rights, due process (Eight and Fourteenth Amendments), for our Civil Rights violations (1983) and the Eighth Amendment. If help will come to us for justice it must come from this new administration out of Washington, DC. Fresh eyes and no <u>bull</u>. If it is possible to get an investigative hearing on the State Officials that abused Pamela, Candace, Rev. Melvin Easily and James Carpenter, and the public and their power, the investigative hearing or the court system on how blacks are sentenced in these courtrooms when it comes to equal justice. Are the judges and District Attorney abusing their power to impose these lengthy sentences? The Lieutenant of the OHP turned

over the glass salt shaker that Pamela Smith was raped with and identified it (obstruction of justice).

9. Homeland Security (Washington, DC) investigated about the abuse of State officials' scam of power scare at the Oklahoma City Capitol in May 2005 (that abuse, the resources of Homeland Security as a way of keeping Pamela Smith from getting a hearing she has requested by some representative (another cover-up by the State).
10. Department of Justice demanded the Attorney General's office to turn over all the Investigative Reports on the cases of Pamela Smith, Candace Rowe and the State Driver Examiner, Don Cochran.

Pamela Smith
PO Box 470261
Tulsa, OK 74146
918-313-1294

January 6, 2009

Dear Ms. Wright / Potter House:

It was a pleasure to speak to you. I pray our God will always keep you and your family "covered."

I would like to share my story with you. Nobody But God. I was in prison, I worked on a work release program called PPWP in 1997. I live in Tulsa, Oklahoma. I was raped by a Department of Public Safety (DPS) State Driver Examiner. Before I was raped there were many other young girls this driver examiner used his authority to abuse for driving test or written test. I was raped to be able to see my family. They would come up to see me and the State Worker would let me know I broke the rules and could get me shipped out of the program. So I needed to bond with my family. I lost 3 sisters (2 while in prison), so I needed to bond with my son, grandson and brother and some close friends that would come see me at the DPS. I knew it was breaking the rules, but what I didn't know was he was going to threaten me with sex, so I would do it all over again to bond with my family. God and family are all you have in life.

I wrote Bishop T.D. Jakes a letter in 1998. I have that letter today. I wrote him from prison asking him to help me and other women being abused by state workers. I wrote Oprah Winfry, Kenneth Copeland, Rev. Jessie Jackson, Johnny Cochran, and many others, only trying to get some help for some wounded ladies, a cry for justice.

I came home in September 2000, begged all law enforcement

to help me, wanted criminal charges placed on this man for me and all the young innocent girls only trying to obtain a written driver test. I begged the District Attorney, I begged the local U.S. Justice Department and went to Washington, wrote many letters with no results. I went before an <u>all white</u> jury twice, a Civil Trial and a Grand Jury, a true miscarriage of justice for me. A white man raped me and I had an all white jury. The Judge was white, the bailiff was white, my attorney was white. No way, not in that courtroom, evidence was strong. I had a past and I was the wrong color. Lost that battle, but God reminded me it was not over, I couldn't believe the injustice on that case. I was raped with a glass salt shaker at the time.

February 11, 2004 I went to see the District Attorney to beg again to please charge this man with rape, soliciting sex from a minor and rape on an inmate. It is illegal to have sex with an inmate. It is called rape. I couldn't consent to anything. I was a ward of the State of Oklahoma. The District Attorney didn't help. So I went home and I did what I always do, seek God for answers and order my footsteps. God put it on my heart to do a Grand Jury. I never in my life knew how to begin but God did. I called a lawyer and he wanted money which I didn't have, and told me all the reasons I shouldn't do the Grand Jury. I refused to receive his negative advice and told him I didn't care how hard it is to go out and get 8,000 signatures to convene the Grand Jury. I said to that lost soul of an attorney, "You don't know who my God is". Well, I got the petition drawn up and went to the street. I went to some churches. I went to every donkey and pony show I could to get those legally registered voters in Tulsa County. I went to Friendship Baptist Church, Rev. Wendell Tisdale, to get signatures. I had spoken there about my prison abuse so I had a table set up after church and when I was sitting there a lady minister walked up to me and helped me tell people, "Hi, my name is Pamela Smith. I was raped, threatened and tortured with a glass salt shaker. Could you please sign my petition so I can bring in a Grand Jury to investigate this case that the District Attorney chose not to?" So when the minister at Friendship heard me say that, she said, "Oh, my God, you are the lady that the Potter House has been trying to find." She said the Potter House minister called us, which was the Fitzgerald. She said, "I had no idea it was you until now." I said, "Are you kidding me?" She said, "No, I'm so sorry."

I had written the Bishop in 1998, and it was now 2004 when I found out he did answer my cry for help. I thought he didn't care about us, he ignored me like the others, didn't answer my cry, but God had to allowed me to go to the streets to do the Grand Jury, because had Bishop helped me and other victims, then I wouldn't have the story today to tell. God had to have me go through the wilderness, hell, climb mountains, but He needed to expose the devil where it will be He that gets the Glory, not me. He promised me He would expose them and His word did not come back void. I didn't really understand how God was going to fix it, but only in His time. He said, "Pamela, the world will know your story, the one the Oklahoma press hid from the public." I will get the victory. God allowed me to tell the story. I wrote a book called *Begging for Justice, the Silent Coalition.* Now here is how God will expose them; my book will be in all Barnes & Nobles, Borders, and on Amazon.com. Now devil, you can't stop me. This story belongs to God. I was the clay and He the potter. He has made me the strong woman I am today. My book will be out in late February or early March. A true story.

All the time I was disappointed in the Bishop. The devil could see that one day God would use me for glorifying His name.

I'll send a signed copy to you, Ms. Wright, and the Bishop and First Lady. My book will not be out until the end of February. You can find my story on the Internet, <u>Pamela Smith v. the State of Oklahoma & Don Cochran</u>.

Sincerely,

Pamela Smith
PS Rape Foundation

e-mail: psrapefoundation@yahoo.com
website: www.pamelasmith4u.com

PS/ic

CHRONOLOGY

1979 – Trooper #295, James Carpenter, reported sexual misconduct started to highlight itself within the DPS, that inmates were being raped and abused. Trooper Carpenter was fired from his job at OHP where he had been a trooper for many years. In turn he lost his good name when the State of Oklahoma falsely accused him of interfering with another agency's case. The fact is, he is black and he reported what he knew about other rape cases before Pamela Smith and solicited sex from Candace Rowe.

September 1997 – Candace Rowe, written test at school. Requested by State Driver Examiner to come the next day to retest at DPS.

September 1997 – 36th Street North DPS locked victim in room and asked for sex. Candace told her friends at school then reported to Tulsa Police at school.

September 1997 – Candace Rowe filed Police report at her school. Told mom but yet grandmother was with her. Scared to tell her grandmother, afraid grandmother would kill or hurt the state worker and did not want grandmother in trouble.

1997 – OHP had Candace Rowe and mother come for Candace to take polygraph, but would not let her mother be present to take the test. Candace was only 15 and the state was hoping she would not take the test, which she didn't, after being intimidated by OHP Tulsa, Oklahoma, Troop Headquarters "B".

November 1997 to May 1998 – Rape on a former Inmate, Pamela Smith. Raped by State Driver's Examiner, 36th Street North, DPS, Tulsa, Oklahoma.

1997 and 1998 – Candace Rowe's mother wrote letter to

DPS requesting some help for her child who had been locked in a room and solicited for sex by Driver Examiner.

1998 – DPS wrote letter back to Floryda Calloway, Candace's grandmother about what action they were going to take.

January 1998 – State Driver Examiner ordered to go to Oklahoma City and do polygraph for Candace Rowe. He failed test. No charges were ever filed on him for soliciting sex from a minor by District Attorney or OHP or Attorney General's office.

January 1998 – Driver Examiner gave Pamela condom. Showed DPS worker condom; he thought it was a joke and laughed in Pamela's face. Asked Pamela if she was going to tell the head supervisor. And she did just that.

January 1998 – Driver Examiner was taking women to the back room. Pamela reported this to the supervisor.

February 6, 1998 – Raped on birthday at 36th Street North with condom State worker gave Pamela to put up for later use. Pamela was always in fear of being shipped away from her family.

February 18, 1998 – Pamela tells head supervisor that Driver Examiner gave her a condom. He also thought it was a joke and said, "What's wrong with this man?" No action at that time was taken for the abuse on Pamela to stop.

April 1998 – Raped with glass salt shaker in DPS storage room by State Driver Examiner that morning before I could go to hospital to see my last dying sister, Elweeder Brannon Ellis.

April 1998 – Easter Sunday my sister died from an overdose of pills. I was at TCC in Tulsa when she died.

May 1998 – Raped. Told DPS workers in Jenks that Driver Examiner was doing things; not nice to me in DPS Told on several occasions and the Driver Examiner was taking women into the back storage room "not for driver test".

June 1998 – Driver Examiner took Smith and another female to O'Brien Park where he was hugging on the other lady; she was standing between his legs. He endangered the inmate by violating her to be a target to be harmed. He was calling this female from DPS at her house to meet with her. He also gave her flowers and he's a married man.

July 1998 – DPS Supervisor had me alone with another inmate to map out the trip to the park where Driver Examiner picked up the other female. The other inmate was working at DPS that day. She was out for the ride to take us back to the TCC center.

July 1998 – No rape. Driver Examiner was moved away from me to DPS in Jenks. My rape finally stopped after the park trip. I told the Head Supervisor.

August 1998 – No rape. Moved to Jenks. Supervisor moved Driver Examiner away from me.

August 30, 1998 – Returned back to EWCC, Taft, Oklahoma. TCC doors closed – condemned.

September 1998 – Told case manager, Carmilla Clincy, about being raped at DPS. She reported it to Head Supervisor of DPS in Jenks, Oklahoma.

September 1998 – Case manager called medical to get Pamela medical help; declined request at the time by medical. It took months before I could get medical help and a rape kit was never done on me.

September 1998 – Deputy Warden told another DOC worker to write up Case Manager, Carmilla Clincy for believing Smith over DPS worker.

September 1998 – Case manager called a psychiatrist who immediately saw Ms. Smith for months for therapy until she left EWCC. Wrote District Attorney two letters for criminal charges. No help.

October 13, 1998 – This was the beginning of the major cover up by DOC and DPS.

October 13, 1998 – Deputy Warden ordered a polygraph by DOC employee. Deputy Warden, and the DOC Investigator, a faulty polygraph, DOC presented fake ID to come on the grounds to do the faulty test designed by Deputy Warden and the DOC Investigator. Stated he must have picked up the wrong I.D.

October 19, 1998 – Pamela Smith met Deputy Warden on the grounds and asked her, "What was DOC going to do to help me?" Deputy Warden's words were, "You failed the polygraph and if you don't have no one to witness the state driver's examiner raping you, then we are closing the case." I said, "I didn't know you need a witness when you've been raped."

October 19, 1998 – Letter to Oprah Winfrey asking for her help to stop prison rape and to get the story out the gate, because so many rape cases have been covered up at EWCC – many rapes on the grounds.

October 31, 1998 – I saw the Warden at the gym and told her I needed her help. She said she couldn't get into it. She was biased. "But if, Ms. Pamela Smith, you are telling the truth then I indeed believe you are." Then she said, "Fight. How does an inmate fight behind the walls?" Pamela Smith fought from the prison walls, threatened to lockdown, harassed, shake down. I have witnesses to this conversation.

October 1998 – Wrote District Attorney for criminal charges.

November 1998 – Still seen by psychiatrist, Dr. Hoyer at EWCC.

November 8, 1998 – Wrote T.D. Jakes from prison.

December 16, 1998 – Letter from Regional Director closing the case for both agencies.

December 17, 1998 – Letter comes from OHP Trooper, telling me he would be there to see me, the case was not closed. Now who's zooming who?

December 1998 – Still requesting to get medical on the rape.

January 1999 – OHP Trooper came to see me at EWCC for a statement. The DOC Investigator was present for that interview. I gave a recorded statement and affidavit in Taft, Oklahoma.

January or February 1999 – OHP Trooper brings the glass salt shaker to EWCC for Pamela Smith to identify. He pulled it out of his pocket, a tweed jacket. I lost it. I started crying. I asked the Lieutenant who was he going to give it to the Tulsa District Attorney? I was raped in Tulsa County but was locked up at Taft, Oklahoma, Muskogee County, and I wanted to know what county the evidence was going to. He said he didn't know. I did identify it and it has not been seen since, not even for the trials. Lieutenant left it in his desk drawer, a salt shaker that was shoved up a woman's vagina. What happened to the evidence room? DNA, fingerprints?

February 1999 – Lieutenant sent two more lieutenants from OHP to EWCC and did another polygraph test, body language tape. OHP made the DOC Investigator leave. They knew that DOC was only there to intimidate me. I passed that test. I was asked what the investigator and warden did to me at the warden's office, concerning that first faulty polygraph test? I told them, a practice test and the DOC polygraph man asked if he stuck his "dick" in me, and told me what answer to say, yes or no. This test is the one they took in the District Attorney's office to close the case. This one by DOC not DPS. Lieutenant had the glass salt shaker and OHP polygraph test (see the cover up).

February 1999 – The DOC Investigator called me over to his office and asked me if I passed the test for DPS. I told him none of his business. Why doesn't he ask DPS. He said they wouldn't talk to him. I said you have a pipeline to call them. I refused to tell him. I left his office and went back to work at the prison beauty shop for Esther Vaughn and I told her what had happened. DPS Investigator was upset with DOC how they didn't tell them about the case. I wrote a letter asking DPS to come see about me and other rape cases at Taft, Oklahoma, not at Department of Correction.

March 1999 – Regional Director of DOC was on the grounds at EWCC. I went up to him and asked him why he closed my case. He said he was told by his boss at that time. Was DOC Director saying that DPS told them to close the case? That was a lie. Then why did DPS send a letter to me that they were coming to visit me about the rape case against the DPS State Driver Examiner? He asked me if I had a copy of the letter. I said I sent it to my attorney and it was sent to the District Attorney. How could you speak for another agency? He wasn't aware I had been in touch with OHP – more cover up.

May 1999 – My son got married, Maurice and Lesia. I recall crying and so happy but yet sad that I put myself in this situation that kept me from the most important time of my son's life. But I made it up through my wedding. All of them were in mom's wedding, September 7, 2002, Maurice, Lesia and Kyante and family; big brother gave me away.

May 1999 – Tort claim filed by attorney on my behalf.

May 1999 – My attorney called DOC about me not getting medical help on the rape case.

May 1999 – The warden came to me and asked me why I lied about my medical. I said I have not seen the doctor, "I'm not lying. Medical has not seen about me. Gave me some cream but never a rape kit was done on me or for me." The warden didn't know that DPS had been on her grounds. I had to tell her what she didn't know, that the warden was out of the loop on the investigation by her staff not telling her the truth about the case.

July 1999 – New warden came to EWCC. The old one was shipped to Hominy, Oklahoma. Then my medical help came by Ms. Vicki Shoecraft.

January 2000 – Civil suit filed in Northern District Court, Tulsa, Oklahoma.

September 8, 2000 – I came home, worked at the hospital, paid off court costs and fines.

May 7, 2001 – Defendant tried to get Summary Judgment. My attorney and I were ready for trial after the State lost Summary Judgment the Assistant Attorney General told my attorney, she wanted off the case and she knew he was guilty.

May 7, 2001 – My attorney filed a Protective Order in District Court against the State and Attorney for threatening three old ladies at EWCC if they came to Federal Court and testified on Pamela's behalf. They could lose their jobs with DOC. DPS lied that I bragged about stealing five thousand dollars cash from an old lady. Another one of their fabulous lies created by the State of Oklahoma. Said this to an all white jury at civil trial and they fell for that made-up lie.

October 1, 2001 – Worked for Tulsa County Courthouse, cleaned judge's and sheriff's office until the death of my brother, Leon Brannon, a Dallas Policeman, December 13, 2002.

August 12, 2003 – Ruling for Smith. New law established in 10th Circuit Court for inmates. A major victory. Smith v Cochran, Denver, Colorado. Case #00-CV-0035-CS. This case was a piece of history for Pamela Smith, her own cited case in the law books.

December 2003 – State offered $60,000.00 to settle case. I met my attorney at her office along with my brother and another attorney. I declined the $60,000.00. I said, "No, I want to go to court." My attorney was not pleased, she wanted me to take the offer. She said I could end up with an empty judgment if I go to trial.

2004 – Numerous letters written and phone calls to the FBI asking for help. U.S. Department of Justice in Washington, DC letter was received by agency on October 15, 2004.

2004 – Pamela Smith, her husband and another friend met with the FBI in Tulsa, Oklahoma about prosecuting Driver Examiner and seeing if my Civil Rights were violated and to the FBI that the Supervisor lied in Federal Court in January 2004 about an interview with Candace Rowe and her family that never happened.

2004 – Made the first police report on case. No DOC or DPS and OHP made a report. Pamela was an inmate and couldn't call the police to make report. She was awarded to the State of Oklahoma. State President NAACP had me file the report. After all those years no agency made one on her behalf. I can't consent to sex. I can't make the DOC people follow the law. Rape on an inmate is a crime called R.A.P.E.

January 6-13, 2004 – Civil Trial – Smith v. Cochran and DPS. All white jury. Case #00-CV-0035-CS, Tulsa, Oklahoma, Northern District.

February 2004 – I wrote Oprah again because I wanted her to expose prison rape. When I left prison the rapes didn't stop.

February 10, 2004 – Talked to Senator Horner and asked her to call District Attorney and see if we could get criminal charges on their man that raped me. Senator called and was told that the District Attorney himself could not find my case. The Senator told the District Attorney she would have me call him and give him the information on the rape case.

February 10, 2004 – Between 4:30 and 5 o'clock I called the District Attorney. We talked. I told him my name and my case of being raped by a State Driver Examiner. He stated he could not find my name or my case. I told him I had written him letters asking for his help in 1998 and 1999 from prison. He asked if I could bring the letters to him so he could see them. I said yes.

February 11, 2004 – I met with the District Attorney and showed him the letters I wrote asking for charges on the State Driver Examiner that repeatedly raped and abused me at the Driver Examiner's place. The District Attorney asked me if I could get the glass salt shaker. I said no. He said he needed that. There were other conversations with him. I told him that was his job not mine and asked me to keep the politics out of this case.

February 16, 2004 – Made a tape for the Governor of Oklahoma to ask for his help. No response.

February 2004 – Wrote more letters to U.S. Justice

Department, Tulsa and Washington, DC and sent document. Returned back to me, tainted, the Department of Justice case so help wouldn't come to Candace and me.

June 2004 – First Grand Jury Petition. Not enough signatures, Tulsa County for first Grand Jury.

July 2004 – Candace Rowe and Pamela Smith met for the first time. A joyous time. I was happy to meet this strong lady that fought for me and other victims. Pamela is a strong woman (Candace Rowe's words).

August 2004 – Second Grand Jury Petition, Pamela Smith and Candace Rowe, Tulsa County. Smith and Rowe gather signatures all over Tulsa County, sometimes until midnight, even in the extreme heat.

August 2004 – Smith and Rowe do interview at Oklahoma Senator's house and Fox 23 covers it for us. They reported the news and we truly appreciate Fox 23. They were not trying to be the news but let us be the news.

2004 – Smith and Rowe have a "speak out" on rape and soliciting sex at Friendship. A dinner for Minister, Fox 23 covers event.

2004 – Smith and Rowe go to court to hear that they have collected all 5,000 signatures and more necessary to convene the Grand Jury. Candace Rowe read all 10 witness to be called to court. None were called. Pamela Smith gave 65 witnesses and none were called to the Grand Jury. We went to the Grand Jury without an attorney. We were seated before, again, an all white jury – no blacks. Witnesses were called but all from the State. Not even Senator Horner or my doctor. Some were telephoned, designated by the Grand Jury Investigator and the ill advised.

2004 – Candace Rowe's first letter to the FBI, Tulsa.

2004 – Candace Rowe sent letter to the Judge for DPS supervisor saying he talked to her grandmother and mother which is a lie. They never met this DPS supervisor. He lied in court that he talked to her family. More lies in Federal Court about her case against DPS Driver Examiner, an interview that never happened by DPS Head Supervisor.

November 22, 2004 – Grand Jury – "no attorney" – all white jury. Candace Rowe had ten witnesses, none were called to Grand Jury. Pamela Smith had sixty-five witnesses; four were telephoned by the Investigator Assistant; none of the others were called, not even Ms. Smith's doctor. The doctor was asked by phone if his medical records were real. A Grand Jury lady told me that if I didn't have another victim the Driver Examiner did the "same" thing to, they couldn't pass this to the next court. They were given ill advice. I asked the Judge if he and I could have a meeting with the Grand Jury. He met with them, I wrote a request to him about the Jury. No indictment on the State Driver Examiner. The Grand Jury was a joke and I believe they were given ill advice. A Grand Jury indicts a ham sandwich. We were robbed of justice. Our legal system has broken the trust in people to come clean. This State case needs to break up the "Boys' Club" in Oklahoma.

May 2005 – Pamela Smith, husband and a Civil Rights leader met with the Southern Christian Leadership Conference (SCLC) in Atlanta, Georgia, hoping for an investigative hearing on the case. Several members were present. Left documents and a video tape Smith made for the Governor of Oklahoma which he never responded to.

May 2005 – Pamela Smith, husband and a Civil Rights leader went to Oklahoma City to deliver documents on the rape case that was requested by two State House Representatives who were going to try and help us to have the State investigated on abuse of power. The document we left at the Capitol was sealed. When we were traveling down the highway a call came to Reverend Easiley from his wife that we had power in the bag. The Capitol was shut down, all law enforcement was called. That was another smoke screen from the State to keep the case from getting to the right authority for help. The State Representatives requested the package and knew when we came back from Atlanta we were to bring them the document. Homeland Security was abused when Reverend Easiley tried to get the bag checked, the OHP said it was okay, didn't go through checkpoint that day. The Representatives went to the television station and lied about the package, knowing it was us three that dropped it off at his office. He told the television station it was a courier; he knew better. The Civil Rights leader went to Channel 8 and told the real story. Another part of a cover-up from the State of Oklahoma. There was no powder in those bags, I had them sealed up. A trooper went to the Civil Rights leader's home but never ever came to see me. I went to OHP to see why they would go to the Civil Rights leader's home to scare him off the case.

May 2005 – Pamela Smith started hosting Town Hall meetings for family and friends to come out and talk about the prison abuse and meet with our elected officials.

2005 – Civil Rights leader called District Attorney concerning criminal charges on the Driver Examiner for Pamela Smith and Candace Rowe. (Reverend Melvin Easily)

August 2005 – SCLC to be a guest speaker on the Flight to Criminal Justice in Birmingham, Alabama. The offer was accepted. Pamela Smith and Civil Rights leader from the Schoolhouse to the Jailhouse march with the SCLC.

February 2006 – Met with the Oklahoma City branch NAACP President Roosevelt Milton. Became involved in the case. The State President is a true leader for justice.

2006 – Gave attorney $3,000 to take me to the U.S. Supreme Court. Did not happen. I took him to the Bar Association along with the help of the NAACP Oklahoma City Branch for taking client's money under false pretenses.

January 4, 2007 – Press conference hosted by NAACP Oklahoma City branch on the U.S. Supreme Court Writ, Pamela Smith v. Donald Cochran, Washington, DC Case #06-909.

March 23, 2007 – Letter to Oklahoma Senator requesting a meeting on abuse of power scare under Homeland Security. The meeting was set up for April 5, 2007 from the Oklahoma City NAACP President. Did not happen. Senator was not there. He stated that it was a misunderstanding on the appointment / Washington, DC.

December 19, 2008 – Letter to Pamela Smith-Hathorn from Oklahoma Bar Association denied client $3,000.00 funds after attorney was disbarred and used the client and NAACP to get him disbarred after this attorney was up on soliciting sex from clients and seeking funds for cases he never had intended to file cases or say something different after he received the client's money. Now the Oklahoma Bar played us like a bald head.

December 19, 2008 – I received a letter from the Oklahoma Bar Association. The Client Security Fund Claim against the Oklahoma attorney that took $3,000.00 from Pamela Smith's attorney to represent me at the U.S. Supreme Court, Washington, DC, myself, along with the Oklahoma City Chapter NAACP, Roosevelt Milton and his legal team were subpoenaed by the Bar against this attorney. We were successful in getting him disbarred from practicing, Case #CS08-21. I received this letter after we were told that I could get my money returned. That didn't happen from the Bar. The letter read from the Oklahoma Bar Association:

“Dear Ms. Smith-Hathorn: On this date the Board of Governors of the Oklahoma Bar Association met and considered your claim in the amount of $3,000.00.” Know that the Bar got what they wanted out of us. The letter further reads: “After much consideration, the committee determined that your claim fell outside the Scope of Rules. It was the Board of Governor’s decision to confirm the Client’s Security Fund Committee’s recommendation, that your claim be denied.” Now remember, this is a committee Board of Governors, the same Governor that turned a deaf ear to my cry of being raped by a State Driver Examiner. As you can see, the Good Ole Boy Club is still in session. When does justice ever come? I received an e-mail on my YouTube.com from a reader of it who said that “I don’t have a lot of pity. You should not have broken the law.” I responded, “I am not looking for pity. I am looking for justice. Breaking the law does not constitute rape. When sentence is imposed that is my punishment for the crime. Where in the land does the law state that you are supposed to be raped because you committed a crime? Can you honestly say that you have never broken the law? It may have been minor, or you just didn’t get caught, but should you have been raped after you did wrong? What if the shoe was on the other foot? Think before you speak. Inmates lose their freedom when they go to prison, not their constitutional rights.” I hope you don’t have a daughter or wife or a son. You would see rape doesn’t care if you commit a crime or what gender you are.

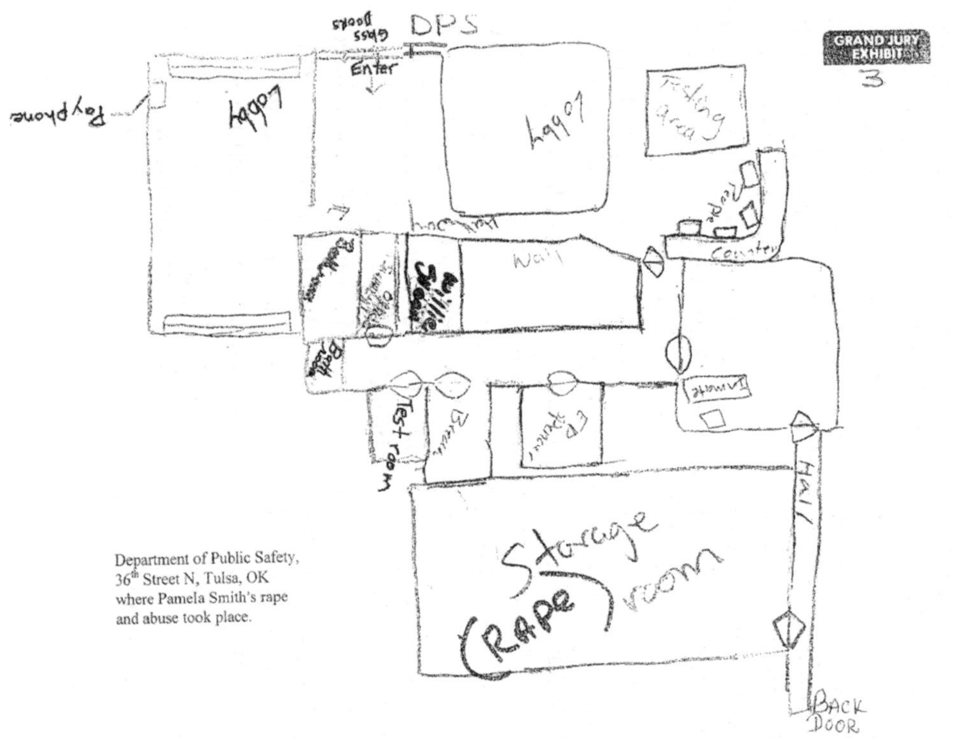

Department of Public Safety,
36th Street N, Tulsa, OK
where Pamela Smith's rape
and abuse took place.

Thank you from the Author, Pamela Smith.

Made in the USA
Middletown, DE
24 June 2021